How to Shop for Food

How to Shop for Food

Practical Tips for the Family Food Buyer

JEAN RAINEY

IN COOPERATION WITH
THE CONSUMER ADVISORY COMMITTEE
OF THE NATIONAL ASSOCIATION OF FOOD CHAINS

BARNES & NOBLE BOOKS

A DIVISION OF HARPER & ROW, PUBLISHERS

New York, Evanston, San Francisco, London

First BARNES & NOBLE BOOKS edition published 1972.

LIBRARY OF CONGRESS CATALOG CARD NUMBER: 75–181602

STANDARD BOOK NUMBER: 06–463340–3

Foreword

Today's supermarkets stock some 8,000 different items. From these you must choose the fifty or so you'll need to feed a family of four for a week. Which are the best buys for you? Which offer good nutrition for your money? Which convenience foods actually cost less than their home-prepared counterparts? How do you select a good cut of meat? How can you stretch your food dollar?

This book was written to help provide answers to these and many other questions today's knowledgeable consumers are asking. It represents the background and practical experience of the Consumer Advisory Committee of the National Association of Food Chains, a committee made up of some twenty-five women who serve supermarket companies as consumer representatives. The information was compiled from literally hundreds of sources in government agencies and the food industry. Their cooperation is gratefully acknowledged.

Authorities don't always agree, so where we found conflicting opinions among our sources, we chose that which we believed most accurate for the typical supermarket situation. Even there, merchandising practices and situations differ from region to region and store to store. Thus, not every supermarket or consumer advisor will agree with everything in this book. We believe it's representative, but fortunately, a competitive industry means differences in practices and attitudes.

Our hope is that this book will help every reader become a better shopper because well-informed shoppers are good customers.

> CLANCY ADAMY, PRESIDENT
> NATIONAL ASSOCIATION OF
> FOOD CHAINS

Contents

How to Shop for Food

CHAPTER 1

Introduction: How This Book Can Help You

Most people think that buying a house is the largest investment they will make during a lifetime, not realizing that they'll probably spend around $80,000 on food. For this is what it can add up to if figured at an average of $25 a week during a lifespan of 17 to 70 and taking into account the number of mouths to be fed at various stages of the family life cycle.

Careful shopping can save you as much as 15 percent of your food budget. Over a lifespan, that can add up to $12,000—enough to build a savings account, put a down payment on a second home, or buy three or four new cars.

This book provides you with the basic information you need to make wise choices in buying food. Knowing what to look for in

selecting from the many kinds of products will make your shopping
more efficient, more economical—and more pleasant.

Perhaps you've noticed that the bones in the standard cuts of
beef, veal, lamb, and pork are pretty much alike in shape. If you
can identify seven basic types of bones you'll be able to look at
almost any cut of meat and have a pretty good idea of its tenderness and whether it will provide you with the most meat for your
money. A simple chart shows you how to do this. Other charts
illustrate the retail cuts of beef, veal, lamb, and pork and indicate
where each cut comes from and how to cook it. The meat chapter
in this book also shows how you can get three meals each from
three different cuts and offers rules of thumb to help you estimate
the number of servings a particular cut will give you.

Do you tend to serve the same fruits and vegetables over and
over again because you don't know much about the less familiar
ones? The chapter on produce has a complete glossary of fruits
and vegetables that gives characteristics to look for and instructions
for storing, preparing, and cooking. It also has a month-by-month
listing of fruits and vegetables in plentiful supply when, of course,
they are best in quality and lowest in cost.

You may be able to cut down on milk costs by using the guidelines offered here for choosing from the different types of milk and
milk products. If you're not sure whether you're getting enough
calcium into your diet when you substitute milk products and milk-
based foods for milk itself, you can check the calcium equivalents
given in a table in the dairy products chapter.

You'll also find helpful tips in this book for buying eggs, butter,
and cheese; breads, cereals, rice, and pastas; coffee and tea; and
salad dressings, shortenings, and oils.

Convenience foods, whether canned, frozen, or in cartons, are
becoming more and more widely accepted. Those sold in large
volume are usually not more expensive than their home-prepared
counterparts. For those that do cost more, you'll need to evaluate
their worth to you in saving time and trouble. Guidelines are provided here. You may find the canned foods size chart particularly
useful—it will help you select the right size cans for your needs.

You may already know some of the government inspection and
grade stamps used to mark meat, poultry, dairy products, and

fruits and vegetables, but perhaps you'd like to know just what these quality and grading standards are based on. This information will be found in Chapter 12, along with illustrations of the actual stamps in use. The government is also responsible for the safety of food additives and requires them to be listed on package labels. The functions of commonly used additives are listed in Chapter 11.

Underlying all food buying, of course, is nutrition. To help the consumer select foods that have the maximum food value for their money, the U.S. Department of Agriculture has prepared a daily food guide. This guide divides foods into four groups: the meat group, the vegetable-fruit group, the milk group, and the bread and cereal group. The foods in each group are similar in nutrient content, and the guide indicates the number of servings necessary from each group to maintain good health. The daily food guide will be found in the appendix of this book. The nutrients themselves—proteins, carbohydrates, fats, minerals, and vitamins—are discussed in Chapter 10.

How you plan your food buying will depend on many things, including the time you have available to shop and prepare meals, your storage and cooking facilities, and the amount of home entertaining you do. However, the crucial factors in your food buying plan are your income and the size of your family.

In preparing a realistic food budget you may find it helpful to consult the cost-of-food-at-home chart in the appendix. This chart gives estimates of the cost of food for families of various sizes and age ranges at three cost levels—low, moderate, and liberal. If you have children under six, or if you're 55 or over, your food budget may not be as high as at other times in your family life cycle. From about age six on, food consumption increases steadily until the teen years, which, as everyone knows, are the most expensive of all.

The chart does not, of course, cover nonfood items such as paper products, household supplies, and cigarettes. According to the U.S. Department of Agriculture, nonfood items account for over 20 cents of every dollar spent in supermarkets.

You may find it saves you time and money in the long run if you plan your menus at the same time you make out your shopping list, keeping in mind the weekly specials offered by the stores you patronize. Rather than waste time, energy, and transportation costs by going from store to store to take advantage of each special, pick one or two stores that carry a wide variety of foods that meet your needs at an average reasonable price. Of course, it's a good idea to look at other store ads occasionally to see if it's time for a change.

When making your shopping list, check your supplies of basic items to see whether any are running out. Also, check your refrigerator for leftovers and try to plan a meal around them. List foods by departments so you won't have to double back and forth when you're in the store. Frozen foods, of course, should be last. If, in planning to use a new recipe, you're not sure what size package to buy of a particular ingredient (for example, grated cheese), consult the yields and equivalents chart in the appendix.

Unit pricing, which translates a package price into price per measure, or price per pound or ounce, is a great help in making intelligent comparisons between similar products. However, don't let it lead you to an overemphasis on price itself; the large size may be too large for your needs, or you may just not like the product which unit pricing shows to be priced lowest.

Open dating is another type of information you should take advantage of. Today, more than two-thirds of the supermarkets in the country are open dating a number of perishable products. You are likely to find more open dating on house brands or private labels because supermarket chains can more readily maintain total control over a product they manufacture, distribute, and sell. For national brand manufacturers serving the country out of one or two plants, open dating is more complex. However, you will soon see a number of these products open dated also.

When comparing similar products, you should also take note of the information supplied by nutritional and ingredient labeling. In the spring of 1972 the Food and Drug Administration proposed regulations for nutritional labeling in an effort to encourage a uniform system of identifying nutrients in packaged foods. The food manufacturer or packer can choose to put nutrition information on a label, but if he does provide this information, it must be offered in a specified manner. In effect, the label must declare, on a per-serving basis, the nutrient quantities of protein, fat, carbohydrates, vitamin A, vitamin C, thiamin, riboflavin, niacin, calcium, and iron, and also the caloric content. The listing of other ingredients is optional.

For years, federal and state laws have required the identification of the ingredients in combination foods. Also, certain foods (for example, mayonnaise) have been standardized by FDA, and any producer wishing to call a product by that name must follow a similar recipe and include a minimum (and in some instances, maximum) amount of certain required and optional ingredients. The Food and Drug Administration currently is considering new and extended ingredient labeling regulations, including those covering standardized products.

No matter how wisely you have shopped, your food will be subject to waste and spoilage if you don't store it properly. Storage charts for cupboard, refrigerator, and freezer, to be found in the appendix, give the recommended storage time and advice on handling for all types of items.

How will shopping for food be different in the future? First, new types of products will be available. Just coming on the market, for example, are newly formulated meat substitutes and egg products, usually developed with a soy bean base. There will be many more convenience foods and ready-to-eat meals.

A prospect in the offing is the standardization of federal and state grade or quality criteria. The grades now in use were developed originally to assist farmers in marketing their products. Thus, tradition established meat grades of Prime, Choice, and Good, while apples were designated Extra Fancy, Fancy, and No. 1, and eggs, Grade AA, A, and B. Because the same term stands for different things in different commodities, U.S. No. 1 may be a top rating in one commodity and signify mediocre or below in another. Standardization of grade names would undoubtedly encourage greater use of consumer grade labeling on products.

The metric system of weights and measures will eventually be adopted. Practically all of the world except North America uses it. Conversion will be a gigantic job; when it comes about it will bring changes in traditional sizes and shapes of packages. In the long run, shopping will be simplified, but it may take awhile to get used to buying a liter (1.06 qt.) of milk, a kilogram (2.2 lb.) can of coffee, or a 500 gram (1.1 lb.) loaf of bread.

The automatic checkstand will take the place of the present

check-out counter. Under this system, which makes use of the electronic computer and the optical scanner, packaged items will be moved along a belt past the scanner which will read the code marking and ring up the price on the cash register.

For years there have been predictions of a future in which we will do our own grocery shopping at home via video-telephone. However, not much progress is being made in this direction, perhaps in part because it will be a long time before people are ready to accept a substitute for actually going to the store, finding a steak with just the right thickness, hefting the cabbage to see if it is good and solid, or smelling the cantaloupe for ripeness!

CHAPTER 2

The Meat Department Simplified

Introduction

There's no department in the store where know-how counts more than in the meat department. Up to one-third of the food budget is spent on meat items, including poultry and seafood. If you're spending more than that, perhaps you should take another look at the cuts of meat you're buying and how much you're buying. You may be slighting one of the other basic food groups or concentrating on chops and roasts to the exclusion of some of the other less expensive and equally nutritious cuts.

Dieters tend to think they can eat all the meat they want and control their weight. Meat is valuable for its protein, but it also has calories, and large quantities that can't be burned as energy will result in weight gain, not weight loss.

Price Per Serving, Not Price Per Pound

The first, and most important, rule to remember is that it's not the price per pound but the price per serving that counts. If flank steak (or London broil) is $1.49 a pound, it's a far better buy than short ribs at 69 cents a pound. You'll get four servings at 37 cents each from flank steak but probably only 1 serving from the short ribs at 69 cents.

Start out with these rules of thumb for servings per pound:

Boneless meat. 4 servings per pound. Ground meat, flank steak, round steak, stew meat, liver, center cut of ham, veal cutlet, fish steaks, fillets.

Bone in meat. 2 to 3 servings per pound. Most roasts, some chops and steaks, ham, poultry, and dressed fish.

Meat with substantial fat and bone. 1 to 2 servings per pound. Rib chops of lamb, pork, or veal; rib roast; brisket; plate and breast of lamb or veal; short ribs; spareribs; shank; porterhouse, T-bone and club steaks; chicken wings and backs.

How big is a serving? That really depends on you and your family. Three ounces of cooked lean meat is the most common definition of a meat serving, but 2 ounces is a satisfactory amount and probably just right for small children and older persons with small appetites. To visualize 3 ounces, think of two pieces of meat, each about 4″ x 2″ x ¼″ in size.

If you have a family with hefty appetites, you probably will adjust the suggested "rule of thumb" servings downward to your actual needs. As you grow accustomed to using the price per serving method for buying meat, you'll find you automatically look at a cut and estimate "by eye" how many servings it will give you. To help you get started though, here are some comparative figures based on July 1972 prices.

COST PER SERVING

11 TO 20¢: beef liver, frying chicken, frozen ocean perch fillets, sardines, tuna

21 TO 30¢: lean ground beef, whole ham (cured, ready to cook), picnic shoulder, chicken breast, turkey, frozen haddock fillet

31 TO 40¢: beef chuck roast, canned ham
41 TO 50¢: round steak, pork loin roast, rump roast
51¢ OR MORE: rib roast, sirloin and porterhouse steaks, pork chops, veal cutlets, lamb chops

Buy the Specials

Meat on "special" is usually priced 10 to 30 cents a pound below its regular price. If you have a freezer and the money to invest in the future, you can buy enough to keep for later use.

Take Advantage of Big Cuts of Meat

Paying $4.00 to $5.00 for a big roast or ham may not be the extravagance it seems if you get 12 to 16 servings of freshly cooked meals out of it. Illustrated here are some ideas on how to get three different meals each from a chuck roast, a leg of lamb, and a pork butt. During the summer, especially, when shoppers tend to choose quick-cooking meats, the big cuts move slowly and are attractively priced.

Learn to Use the Less Tender Cuts

Only about one-quarter of the carcass ends up as tender steaks and roasts, which command the highest prices. That leaves three-quarters of the carcass in less tender cuts, which are lower-priced but require more ingenuity from the cook. These cuts are every bit as nutritious and often yield more lean meat per pound because they generally have less fat. It's said that the superb French cuisine developed because it was necessary to stretch limited supplies of less tender meat.

Discover Variety Meats

Most of us know that liver is a bargain, both nutritionally and price-wise, but how long is it since you prepared tongue? Do you ever serve brains, kidneys, sweetbreads, beef heart, or tripe? All these variety meats are highly regarded by gourmets, but too many home cooks shrink from them in disdain. If you're tired of

TIPS FOR CUTTING MEAT AT HOME

Roast, steaks, stew...
from one cut of Beef Chuck

You may not always find this cut—an arm cut or round-bone pot roast—since beef chuck is cut differently in various parts of the country. However, when you do buy a round-bone pot roast, have it cut thick and use it this way. Instead of pot roast on Sunday and hash on Monday and Tuesday, you'll have three fresh-cooked and entirely different meals that you can spread over a week's time.

Meal 1. Beef Stew
From the round end of the roast, cut off a boneless piece of meat to cube for beef stew.

Meal 2. Pot Roast
Cut a piece from the center for a small, one-meal pot roast.

Meal 3. Swiss Steaks
With a sharp knife, you can easily split the remaining piece to make two attractive Swiss steaks. Braise 1 to 2 hours.

How to use a large Leg of Lamb economically

This idea works equally well with a small leg of lamb, but it's especially recommended for use with larger legs of lamb (7 to 9 pounds). This is just one of several good ways to divide a whole (full-cut) leg of lamb so you don't have to cook it all at once.

Meal 1. Lamb Steaks to Broil
Broil the lamb steaks just as you would loin chops. Serve sizzling hot with broiled pineapple slices.

Meal 2. Lamb Roast
Here's your Sunday roast —just the easy-to-carve center portion of the leg. Make a panful of gravy and serve with potatoes and peas. Remember, you'll get more juicy slices and less cooking shrinkage if you roast lamb at a low temperature (no higher than 325° F.).

Meal 3. Stew, Curry or Shish-kebabs
Later in the week, cut the meat from the shank into cubes for another freshly cooked meal. Use these tender, boneless cubes of lamb in an Irish stew—or a more glamorous dish such as lamb curry or shish-kebabs (marinated pieces of lamb grilled on skewers along with green pepper, onions and tomatoes).

SOURCE: *Ideas with Meat.* Chicago: American Meat Institute, pp. 9, 10, and 11.

How to make three fresh-cooked meals from one Pork Butt

The whole fresh pork shoulder butt is a nearly bone-less cut that usually weighs from 5 to 7 pounds. You can easily divide this economical cu at home into a roast, boneless steaks and cubed pork for grinding or casserole dishes.

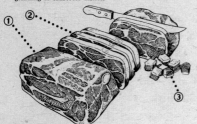

Meal 1. Pork Roast

Cut across the roast as shown to divide it into two pieces. Use the piece with the bone for your pork roast.

Meal 2. Pork Steaks

The remaining piece is clear, solid meat. From it you can cut boneless pork steaks about one-half inch thick. Braise these steaks just as you would pork chops, i. e., brown, then cook in a covered skillet with or without added liquid.

Meal 3. Chop Suey

As you get to the small end of the boneless piece, cut the remaining meat into small cubes. Use the diced pork for a meat-stretching dish of chop suey, or in a casserole.

searching for new recipes for hamburger, look for ways to serve variety meats.

Remember Meat Alternates

In addition to beef, veal, lamb, pork, poultry, fish, and seafood, the meat group includes eggs, cheese, dry beans, peas, lentils, nuts, and peanut butter. All have a high protein content. However, when you use dry beans, peas, lentils, or nuts as alternates to meat, be sure to serve them with milk and cheese or combine with milk, cheese, or small amounts of meat in recipes. They are an incomplete source of protein and should be supplemented by some animal protein.

The following chart gives you information about meat alternatives.

COSTS FOR SIMILAR AMOUNTS OF PROTEIN

Food	Amount ready to eat	Amount purchased	Cost of serving*
Hamburger	2 ounces	⅙ pound	$0.11
Eggs	2	2	.09
Pork and beans	1 cup	½ (1 pound can)	.07
Dry beans	1 cup	3 oz. (dry)	.03
Peanut butter	4 tablespoons	2 oz.	.06
American cheese (processed)	2 slices	¼ (8 ounce package)	.12
	2 ounces	¹⁄₁₆ (2 pound package)	.10
Cottage cheese	½ cup	⅛ (2 pound carton)	.07

SOURCE: *Your Money's Worth in Foods.* Washington, D.C.: U.S. Department of Agriculture, Home and Garden Bulletin No. 183, December 1970, p. 14.

* Costs based on prices in Washington, D.C., supermarkets in June 1970.

Consult your cookbook for different ways to serve meat alternates. For starters, check recipes for egg croquettes, egg foo yung, baked eggs on Spanish rice, quiche, cheese strata, peanut butter rarebit, three-bean casserole, bean chowder, bean burgers, peanut burgers, eggs à la king, and french toast with peanut butter sauce.

Now let's consider the basic meat cuts.

Beef

Marbling, color, and shape and color of the bone are the three characteristics you should "train your eyes" to evaluate in buying beef. There should be a moderate fat covering over most of the exterior, but color of exterior fat is not an indication of quality because it varies with age, breed, and feed. The lean meat should be a uniform, bright, light to deep red. Fine-textured lean meat is preferable to coarse-textured lean meat, and firm, dry lean meat is preferable to soft, moist lean meat.

The exception to the color rule is in "aged beef," that is, beef that has been held at temperatures of 34° to 38° F. for three to six weeks or held for two days at about 70°. In the second method, ultraviolet light is used to reduce bacterial growth. Aging develops additional tenderness and flavor but should not be undertaken at home since it requires controlled conditions. Aged beef will be dark red or almost blue in color; it is usually sold to restaurants.

Bones of younger animals are porous and red, whereas bones of older animals (which will have less tender meat) are white and flinty.

The bones in beef, lamb, veal, and pork are similar in shape, so if you learn to identify the seven different types of bones pictured here, you'll be able to judge a variety of cuts of meat.

Look carefully, for example, at the three different types of blade bones shown. Note that the nearly flat one identifies the blade cut near the rib, the more tender part of the animal. Next time you buy a blade chuck roast, look for the type of bone near the rib for meat that will be more tender.

Now, look at the sirloin bones, especially the pin bone and the wedge bone. Note that the pin bone is near the short loin, the most tender part of the animal, whereas the wedge bone is near the round, a less tender part. Next time you buy a sirloin steak, look for one with the pin bone, which will give you meat closer in eating quality to that of tenderloin steak. On the other hand, if you want the most meat for the money, the wedge bone sirloin is a better buy.

The accompanying beef chart illustrates the retail cuts of beef

BONES IDENTIFY SEVEN GROUPS OF RETAIL CUTS

Shoulder Arm Cuts	Arm Bone		
Shoulder Blade Cuts (Cross Sections of Blade Bone)	Blade Bone (near neck)	Blade Bone (center cuts)	Blade Bone (near rib)
Rib Cuts	Back Bone and Rib Bone		
Short Loin Cuts	Back Bone (T-Shape) T-Bone		
Hip (Sirloin) Cuts (Cross Sections of Hip Bone)	Pin Bone (near short loin)	Flat Bone* (center cuts)	Wedge Bone† (near round)
Leg or Round Cuts	Leg or Round Bone		
Breast, or Brisket Cuts	Breast and Rib Bones		

*Formerly part of "double bone" but today the back bone is usually removed leaving only the "flat bone" (sometimes called "pin bone") in the sirloin steak.

†On one side of sirloin steak, this bone may be wedge shaped while on the other side the same bone may be round.

SOURCE: *Lessons on Meat,* second edition. Chicago: National Live Stock and Meat Board, 1971, p. 35.

and shows where they come from. A little time spent studying this chart and relating it to the bone shapes described above will help you tremendously in buying meat. Note that the most tender cuts of beef come from the center section of the animal, which is least affected by exercise. The chart also indicates the best cooking methods for various cuts.

Many markets sell beef under one or more of three USDA grades, which are an indication of tenderness. The top grade is *Prime*, which identifies meat that is well marbled with flecks of fat within the lean. Most of this is sold to hotels and restaurants, but some stores offer prime beef in addition to the next grade, choice. *Choice* is the predominant grade in most markets because it is satisfactorily tender but has less waste than prime. *Good,* the third grade in order of tenderness, is also offered by some stores to give customers a chance to buy beef at lower cost. Tenderness, of course, has nothing to do with nutrition; good or choice beef will give you just as much or more nutrition for your money because it has less fat than prime.

Beef Steaks

A good steak is the epitome of good eating to many Americans. In order of desirability in terms of tenderness, and priced accordingly, are the tenderloin (filet mignon), porterhouse, T-bone, club steak, and strip or loin steaks. The filet has no bone and very little fat and is all tenderloin. The porterhouse has a generous section of tenderloin which can be removed and served separately as filet. The T-bone is similar to porterhouse but has a smaller section of tenderloin. Next in order are the club and strip or top loin steaks, which have the same large muscle as the porterhouse and T-bone but no tenderloin.

Next in order of tenderness is the sirloin steak, perhaps the most popular steak with families because of its large size. Sometimes you'll find steak labeled top or bottom sirloin. The top is the better of the two. The sirloin tip is a boneless steak which is less tender than the regular sirloin.

Rib and rib eye (also known as Delmonico) steaks are cut from the rib section. The rib steak is sold as rib roast when it has

BEEF CHART

RETAIL CUTS OF BEEF — WHERE THEY COME FROM AND HOW TO COOK THEM

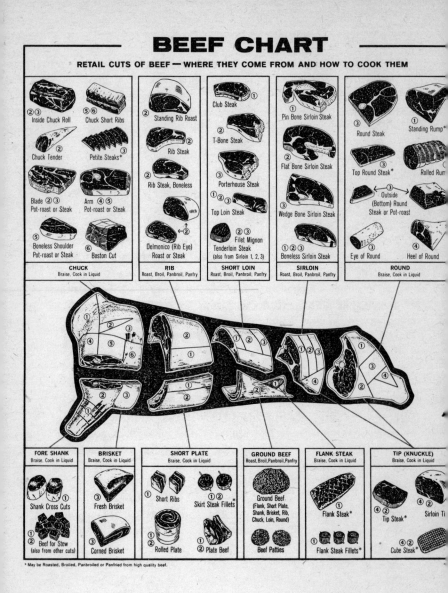

CHUCK	RIB	SHORT LOIN	SIRLOIN	ROUND
Braise, Cook in Liquid	Roast, Broil, Panbroil, Panfry	Roast, Broil, Panbroil, Panfry	Roast, Broil, Panbroil, Panfry	Braise, Cook in Liquid

CHUCK: Inside Chuck Roll ②③, Chuck Short Ribs ⑤⑥, Chuck Tender ②, Petite Steaks* ③, Blade Pot-roast or Steak ②③, Arm Pot-roast or Steak ④⑤, Boneless Shoulder Pot-roast or Steak ⑤, Boston Cut ⑥

RIB: Standing Rib Roast ②, Rib Steak, Rib Steak, Boneless ②, Delmonico (Rib Eye) Roast or Steak ②

SHORT LOIN: Club Steak ①, T-Bone Steak ②, Porterhouse Steak ③, Top Loin Steak ①②③, Filet Mignon Tenderloin Steak ②③ (also from Sirloin 1, 2, 3)

SIRLOIN: Pin Bone Sirloin Steak ①, Flat Bone Sirloin Steak ②, Wedge Bone Sirloin Steak ③, Boneless Sirloin Steak ①②③

ROUND: Round Steak ③, Standing Rump* ①, Top Round Steak* ③, Rolled Rump, Outside (Bottom) Round Steak or Pot-roast, Eye of Round ③, Heel of Round ④

FORE SHANK	BRISKET	SHORT PLATE	GROUND BEEF	FLANK STEAK	TIP (KNUCKLE)
Braise, Cook in Liquid	Braise, Cook in Liquid	Braise, Cook in Liquid	Roast, Broil, Panbroil, Panfry	Braise, Cook in Liquid	Braise, Cook in Liquid

FORE SHANK: Shank Cross Cuts ①, Beef for Stew ② (also from other cuts)

BRISKET: Fresh Brisket ③, Corned Brisket ③

SHORT PLATE: Short Ribs ①, Skirt Steak Fillets ①②, Rolled Plate ②, Plate Beef ①②

GROUND BEEF: Ground Beef (Flank, Short Plate, Shank, Brisket, Rib, Chuck, Loin, Round), Beef Patties

FLANK STEAK: Flank Steak* ①, Flank Steak Fillets* ①

TIP (KNUCKLE): Tip Steak* ④①, Sirloin Tip ④②, Cube Steak* ④②

* May be Roasted, Broiled, Panbroiled or Panfried from high quality beef.

SOURCE: National Live Stock and Meat Board, Chicago.

two or more ribs. The rib eye, or Delmonico, is literally the eye of beef rib and is exceptionally tender.

Many economy-minded families choose chuck steaks, either blade or arm. Blade is the more tender of the two, but both require tenderizing with one of the commercial meat tenderizers or marinating overnight to make them suitable for broiling or a cook-out.

Round steak is another economy steak because it has very little waste. Its lack of marbling means it's not as flavorful or juicy as the others. Top round can be broiled, but bottom round requires moist cooking. Eye of round can be pan-broiled.

Buy steaks at least 1 inch thick if you plan to broil them, especially if you like rare or medium-rare steak. It's hard to get the proper degree of doneness with a thin steak. Thin steaks should be pan broiled.

Beef Roasts

Whether a beef roast should be oven roasted or prepared as a pot roast is a question many shoppers ask as they look at an unfamiliar cut of meat. Following is a brief review of roasts. It indicates which ones can be oven roasted, if they're Prime or Choice grades, and which require moist cooking or "pot roasting."

OVEN ROAST

RIB ROAST: the luxury cut of the roast family, not only because of its tenderness, but also because its large amount of fat and bone means that from ½ to 1 pound of meat must be allowed per person.

RIB EYE: like the rib eye steak, the boneless heart of the rib roast. It has substantially less waste; 3 servings per pound.

RUMP: a flavorful cut, but less tender than the rib; 3 servings per pound.

SIRLOIN TIP: like the sirloin tip steak, not as tender as regular sirloin; 3 servings per pound.

POT ROAST

EYE OF ROUND: less tender than the above cuts, but has good flavor; 3 servings per pound.

HEEL OF ROUND: less tender than the eye of round; 3 servings per pound.

ENGLISH (BOSTON): a square cut of beef containing 2 or 3 rib bones; alternating layers of lean and fat, thicker at one end; 2 servings per pound.

BLADE CHUCK: contains the blade bone, rib bone, and back bone; more tender but also more waste than the arm; 1½ servings per pound.

ARM CHUCK: contains less bone than the blade but is less tender; excellent flavor; 2 servings per pound.

BRISKET: often cured and sold as corned beef, is also sold fresh, usually with bone removed; 2 servings per pound.

Ground Beef

Ground beef, the most popular single item in the meat department, is taken from the flank, short plate, shank, brisket, rib, chuck, loin, and round sections of the carcass. It is limited by law to a maximum fat content of 30 percent. Traditionally, ground meat that is designated as *hamburger* contains the most fat, while *ground chuck* is lean and *ground round* is extra lean. Some supermarkets are now labeling their ground beef with such designations as *ground beef, lean ground beef,* and *extra lean ground beef.* Others have labels which show the percentage of fat or lean in the package of ground beef. You probably have seen such labels as *Approx. 75% lean* or *Approx. 21–25% fat* or *Approx. 81–85% lean.* Again, the price will reflect the cost of the lean beef content, and it's up to you to decide whether you prefer the lower-priced regular ground beef, and the juicy hamburgers it produces, or the higher-priced lean variety.

Veal

Mention the word "veal" and most people think of veal cutlets, but there are many cuts which offer the same delicate flavor for less money. Veal prices do not vary as much as beef prices but tend to be lower in spring and summer and higher in winter.

Meat from calves up to six months of age is generally considered as veal. Look for meat that is light grayish pink in color with a very fine grain and that is fairly firm and velvety in texture. Bones are porous and red, and only a small amount of fat is found.

Because the cuts are similar to those in beef, there is no need to discuss them in detail. The accompanying veal chart shows you where the most desirable cuts are.

Most veal cuts, except those in the tender middle section, will benefit from moist cooking because veal has so little fat.

If you enjoy such dishes as veal parmigiano or veal scaloppine, consider buying a veal rump, leg, or sirloin roast, which generally are lower priced than the highly-prized cutlets, and then slicing it into ¼ inch thick slices, about 2 or 3 inches square. The slicing may not take much more time than pounding the cutlet thin. About half the roast will slice nicely; the remainder can be cubed for any one of a variety of veal casseroles or veal-in-a-sauce dishes.

In addition to the cuts shown in the chart, consider these possibilities: veal drumsticks—ground veal shaped like a chicken leg around a wooden skewer; veal birds—very thin sliced boneless veal; and city chicken—veal cubes threaded on a skewer.

Lamb

Lamb is meat from young sheep, usually less than a year old. Very few sheep are marketed in this country, but if you see the label *yearling mutton,* it identifies meat coming from sheep between one and two years old. Older sheep are sold as *mutton.*

In buying lamb, remember that the darker the lean meat, the older the animal. Very young milk-fed lamb meat is light pink and lean; spring lamb is darker pink; older, high quality lambs have light red lean meat. The bones in older lambs will appear drier, harder, and less red than the bones of younger lambs. Look for firm, fine-textured lean meat and firm fat. As with beef, the color of fat varies and is not an indicator of quality.

The chart of bone sizes illustrated earlier in this chapter will also serve as a guide for buying lamb. The accompanying lamb chart is offered for study, too, and gives the cooking methods recommended for the various cuts.

The days of being limited to spring lamb are gone, and flavorful

VEAL CHART

RETAIL CUTS OF VEAL — WHERE THEY COME FROM AND HOW TO COOK THEM

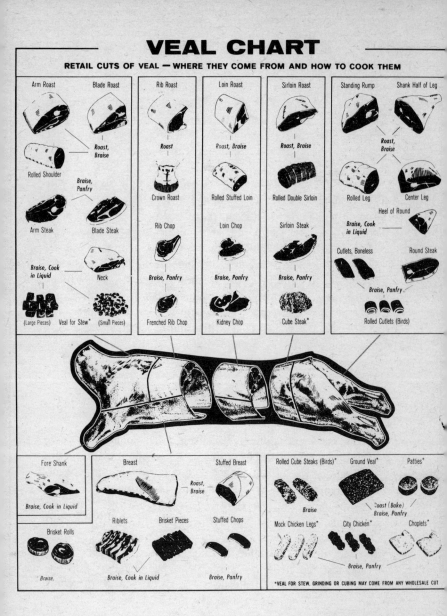

Arm Roast　　**Blade Roast**

Rolled Shoulder

Roast, Braise

Braise, Panfry

Arm Steak　　**Blade Steak**

Neck

Braise, Cook in Liquid

(Large Pieces)　Veal for Stew　(Small Pieces)

Rib Roast

Roast

Crown Roast

Rib Chop

Braise, Panfry

Frenched Rib Chop

Loin Roast

Roast, Braise

Rolled Stuffed Loin

Loin Chop

Braise, Panfry

Kidney Chop

Sirloin Roast

Roast, Braise

Rolled Double Sirloin

Sirloin Steak

Braise, Panfry

Cube Steak*

Standing Rump　　**Shank Half of Leg**

Roast, Braise

Rolled Leg　　**Center Leg**

Heel of Round

Braise, Cook in Liquid

Cutlets, Boneless　　**Round Steak**

Braise, Panfry

Rolled Cutlets (Birds)

Fore Shank

Braise, Cook in Liquid

Brisket Rolls

Braise.

Breast　　**Stuffed Breast**

Roast, Braise

Riblets　**Brisket Pieces**　**Stuffed Chops**

Braise, Cook in Liquid　　*Braise, Panfry*

Rolled Cube Steaks (Birds)*　**Ground Veal***　**Patties***

Braise

Roast (Bake) Braise, Panfry

Mock Chicken Legs*　**City Chicken***　**Choplets***

Braise, Panfry

*VEAL FOR STEW, GRINDING OR CUBING MAY COME FROM ANY WHOLESALE CUT

SOURCE: National Live Stock and Meat Board, Chicago.

LAMB CHART

RETAIL CUTS OF LAMB — WHERE THEY COME FROM AND HOW TO COOK THEM

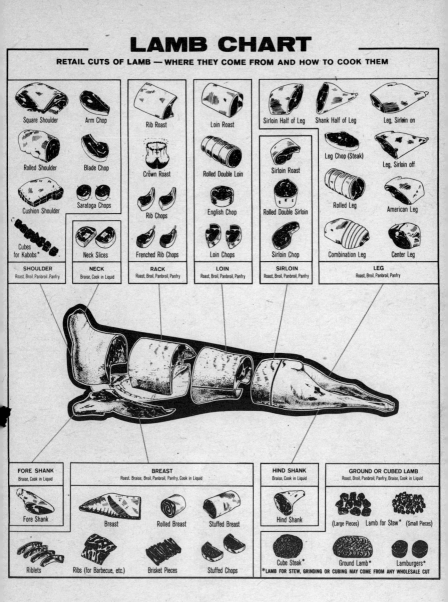

Square Shoulder	Arm Chop
Rolled Shoulder	Blade Chop
Cushion Shoulder	Saratoga Chops
Cubes for Kabobs*	

Rib Roast

Crown Roast

Rib Chops

Frenched Rib Chops

Loin Roast

Rolled Double Loin

English Chop

Loin Chops

Sirloin Half of Leg | Shank Half of Leg | Leg, Sirloin on

Sirloin Roast

Rolled Double Sirloin

Sirloin Chop

Leg Chop (Steak)

Leg, Sirloin off

Rolled Leg

American Leg

Combination Leg | Center Leg

Neck Slices

SHOULDER
Roast, Broil, Panbroil, Panfry

NECK
Braise, Cook in Liquid

RACK
Roast, Broil, Panbroil, Panfry

LOIN
Roast, Broil, Panbroil, Panfry

SIRLOIN
Roast, Broil, Panbroil, Panfry

LEG
Roast, Broil, Panbroil, Panfry

FORE SHANK
Braise, Cook in Liquid

Fore Shank

Riblets

BREAST
Roast, Braise, Broil, Panbroil, Panfry, Cook in Liquid

Breast | Rolled Breast | Stuffed Breast

Ribs (for Barbecue, etc.) | Brisket Pieces | Stuffed Chops

HIND SHANK
Braise, Cook in Liquid

Hind Shank

GROUND OR CUBED LAMB
Roast, Broil, Panbroil, Panfry, Braise, Cook in Liquid

(Large Pieces) Lamb for Stew* (Small Pieces)

Cube Steak* | Ground Lamb* | Lamburgers*

*LAMB FOR STEW, GRINDING OR CUBING MAY COME FROM ANY WHOLESALE CUT

SOURCE: National Live Stock and Meat Board, Chicago.

lamb is now available the year round. However, demand will still set prices. Leg of lamb and lamb chops are the most popular cuts, but don't overlook such delicious possibilities as roast lamb shoulder, either square cut or boned and rolled. Or try curried lamb or lamb shish kebabs, both made from cubes cut from the shoulder or leg.

Nearly all lamb cuts are tender enough to be cooked without added liquid. They can be roasted, broiled, pan broiled, or pan fried, but for variety, they are delicious simmered or braised. And remember that lamb cooked by any method tastes best if served piping hot or chilled, rather than warm.

Pork

Pork is meat from pigs or hogs, usually under one year of age. Young pork has grayish-pink lean meat, whereas older animals yield lean meat that is rose pink in color. Look for firm, fine-grained flesh, free of excessive moisture. The lean should be well marbled and covered with firm white fat.

Pork is sold fresh, cured, or cured and smoked. High in nutritive value, it is an especially rich source of thiamin (Vitamin B_1).

The new pork of the 70s is a vastly different product from that of earlier years. Scientific breeding of a new meat-type hog and closer trimming of fat by both meat packers and retailers means leaner meat, comparable in calorie value to beef and veal. The leaner quality makes it easier to digest, too.

Along with the new pork have come new pork cookery methods. Careful research studies over the past 10 years show that cooking pork roasts (loin, shoulder, and leg) to the new 170° F. internal temperature, rather than the old 185° F., produces an equally desirable and juicier end product. In addition to the bonus of less cooking time, there's less waste due to shrinkage during cooking.

Just as with other types of meat, bone size and shape are keys to buying pork. Study the pork chart here for indicators, and remember the bone types described earlier in the chapter. As with beef, the most desirable cuts are those from the loin. Loin chops

PORK CHART

RETAIL CUTS OF PORK — WHERE THEY COME FROM AND HOW TO COOK THEM

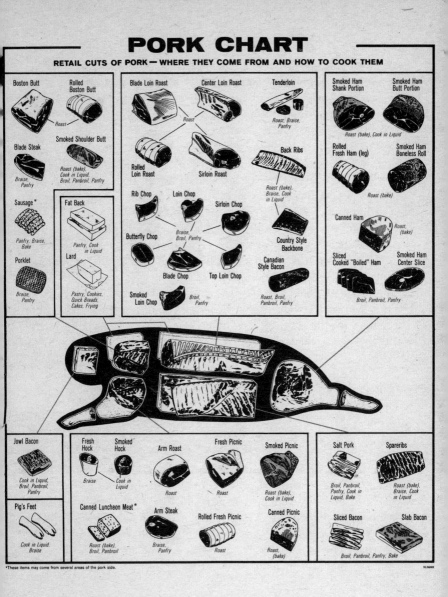

Boston Butt — Roast

Rolled Boston Butt

Blade Steak — Braise, Panfry

Smoked Shoulder Butt — Roast (bake), Cook in Liquid, Broil, Panbroil, Panfry

Sausage * — Panfry, Braise, Bake

Porklet — Braise, Panfry

Fat Back — Panfry, Cook in Liquid

Lard — Pastry, Cookies, Quick Breads, Cakes, Frying

Blade Loin Roast — Roast

Center Loin Roast — Roast

Rolled Loin Roast

Sirloin Roast

Rib Chop

Loin Chop

Sirloin Chop

Butterfly Chop — Braise, Broil, Panfry

Blade Chop

Top Loin Chop

Smoked Loin Chop — Broil, Panfry

Tenderloin — Roast, Braise, Panfry

Back Ribs — Roast (bake), Braise, Cook in Liquid

Country Style Backbone

Canadian Style Bacon — Roast, Broil, Panbroil, Panfry

Smoked Ham Shank Portion

Smoked Ham Butt Portion — Roast (bake), Cook in Liquid

Rolled Fresh Ham (leg)

Smoked Ham Boneless Roll — Roast (bake)

Canned Ham — Roast, (bake)

Sliced Cooked "Boiled" Ham

Smoked Ham Center Slice — Broil, Panbroil, Panfry

Jowl Bacon — Cook in Liquid, Broil, Panbroil, Panfry

Pig's Feet — Cook in Liquid, Braise

Fresh Hock — Braise

Smoked Hock — Cook in Liquid

Canned Luncheon Meat * — Roast (bake), Broil, Panbroil

Arm Roast — Roast

Arm Steak — Braise, Panfry

Fresh Picnic — Roast

Rolled Fresh Picnic — Roast

Smoked Picnic — Roast (bake), Cook in Liquid

Canned Picnic — Roast, (bake)

Salt Pork — Broil, Panbroil, Panfry, Cook in Liquid, Bake

Sliced Bacon

Spareribs — Roast (bake), Braise, Cook in Liquid

Slab Bacon — Broil, Panbroil, Panfry, Bake

*These items may come from several areas of the pork side.

SOURCE: National Live Stock and Meat Board, Chicago.

may be considered the T-bone steaks of pork, while rib chops are similar to club or strip steaks in beef in that they do not have the tenderloin section. Tenderness is not the main factor in buying pork, as it is in beef, because all pork comes from young animals and thus is tender.

Boston butt is comparable to a blade chuck roast in beef, and the arm roast is comparable to the beef arm chuck roast. When either is sliced, the result is known as blade steaks and arm steaks. Fresh picnics might be compared to the English or Boston cut in beef.

Center-cut pork chops, which command premium prices, are taken from the center of the loin. The remainder is sold as rib-end or loin-end roasts or chops. Although rib-end roasts are sold at substantially lower prices, studies made at Cornell University suggest that you'll get more meat for your money by buying the loin end and having it sliced for pork chops, even if your store charges for this service. The loin-end chops will have as much meat as the center-cut chops at a price which may be 5 to 7 cents less per chop. The study also suggests that, despite the waste they contain, the sliced rib-end chops are often a better buy than the center-cut chops because you will usually get two chops for about the price of one center-cut chop.

Cured Pork

Cured or smoked pork—ham, bacon, and so on—comes in so many different forms these days that you must always read the label to find the content. *Cured* means the pork has been treated with curing ingredients—salt, sodium or potassium nitrate, and/or nitrite, and sugar. *Smoked* is terminology which can be used only on those hams and bacons that have been submitted to actual smoke. Artificial or natural smoke flavoring must be identified on the label.

Be sure to watch for the words *cooked, fully cooked,* or *ready to serve* on ham labels. *Cooked* simply means the ham has been heated during the curing process, but unless the label says *fully cooked* or *ready to serve,* the meat requires further cooking. Of course, many people like to bake and glaze even the fully cooked ham to make it taste and look better.

What does the term *water added* mean? If curing results in an increase in weight of up to 10 percent, federally inspected meat plants are required to label the pork with those words. If it's more than 10 percent, the ham must be labeled *imitation*.

You also will find long-cured or aged hams at the meat counter. After curing these hams are heavily smoked and then aged to develop a distinctive flavor. During aging the hams also shrink in weight. Probably the best known are those produced in Smithfield, Virginia—the famous Smithfield hams. These hams are *long-cut*— that is, they include part of the sirloin region normally left on the loin. They also have long shanks, and very little of the skin and fat are removed from the outside. Smithfield hams should be considered in the luxury class, not only for the price, but because they require more complex preparation.

Bacon varies considerably in flavor and amount of fat and lean. Slab bacon, if available, is probably the best buy. If you prefer sliced bacon, you can choose among thin-sliced, thick-sliced, country style, or canned sliced bacon. Also, consider ends and pieces particularly if you're buying bacon for use in casseroles, sandwiches, or salads.

Don't forget Canadian-style bacon. It is made from boned, trimmed pork loin roast and tastes much like ham. Look for it in a one-pound roll for slicing as needed, or buy it already sliced in a see-through package. Follow the label directions in cooking because many brands are fully cooked.

Remember to save bacon drippings (stored in a jar in the refrigerator) for sautéing meat, scrambling eggs, or mixing in salad dressings. The distinctive smoky flavor of the bacon remains in the drippings, and using them is one economy measure to which few families will object.

Variety Meats

For the uninitiated, here's a list of the different types of variety meats. As with other cuts, there is a similarity among the meats coming from beef, veal, lamb, and pork. In most cases, the size is consistent with the size of the animal, with beef being the largest and lamb the smallest, and veal and pork in between.

Variety Meats for Your Menus

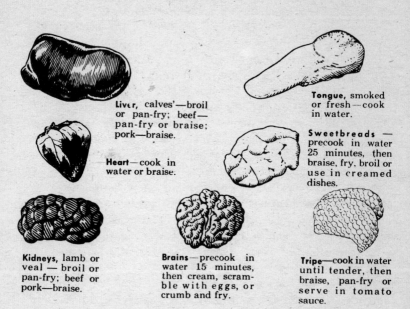

Liver, calves'—broil or pan-fry; beef— pan-fry or braise; pork—braise.

Tongue, smoked or fresh—cook in water.

Heart—cook in water or braise.

Sweetbreads — precook in water 25 minutes, then braise, fry, broil or use in creamed dishes.

Kidneys, lamb or veal — broil or pan-fry; beef or pork—braise.

Brains—precook in water 15 minutes, then cream, scramble with eggs, or crumb and fry.

Tripe—cook in water until tender, then braise, pan-fry or serve in tomato sauce.

SOURCE: *Ideas with Meat*. Chicago: American Meat Institute, p. 7.

Liver. Veal liver is the highest priced, followed by calf (or baby beef) liver, lamb liver, beef liver, and pork liver. Veal, calf, and lamb liver are all mild flavored and tender. Beef liver is less tender. Pork liver has a more pronounced flavor and is less tender but is just as rich a source of iron, vitamin A, and B vitamins as high-priced veal and calf liver.

Heart. Of the four kinds, veal is considered the most delicate in flavor and the most tender. You'll get eight to ten servings from a beef heart, two or three servings from veal heart, two servings from pork heart, and one serving from lamb heart. Heart is very flavorful but needs moist cooking as it is not as tender as other variety meats.

Sweetbreads. This delicate, tender meat is the two lobes of the thymus gland. Veal and young beef furnish nearly all the sweetbreads on the market. As the animal matures, the thymus gland disappears. If sweetbreads are not to be used immediately, they should be precooked before refrigerating and used within 24 hours.

Brains. Like sweetbreads, brains offer tender, delicate meat. Brains also require precooking if they are not used immediately.

Tongue. This may be purchased fresh, pickled, corned, smoked, or canned. The most popular form is smoked beef tongue. Lamb and pork tongues usually are sold in jars and have been cooked, skinned, and boned, and are ready to serve. Tongue requires long, slow cooking, but the flavor makes it worth the effort.

Tripe. This is the inner lining of the beef stomach. There are three kinds: honeycomb, pocket, or plain (smooth), of which honeycomb is considered the greatest delicacy. Tripe also may be purchased fresh, pickled, or canned. It has a delicate flavor and requires long, slow cooking. Tripe is partially cooked before it is sold, but further cooking is preliminary to all ways of serving it.

Kidneys. Veal and lamb kidneys may be sautéed or broiled. Beef kidneys are less tender and require moist cooking.

Sausage Meats

There are literally hundreds of different kinds of meat covered by the broad term "sausage," ranging from the all-American hot dog to breakfast pork sausage and sandwich meats. The term includes any kind of ground, minced, or chopped and spiced meat that is stuffed into casings, shaped into loaves, or simply left loose to be formed into patties.

Because every manufacturer has his own treasured recipe for making sausages, you will want to try different brands to find the one you like best.

If cold meats are on your shopping list, the big factor is whether you're shopping for one or two or for a family of four or more. For the small family, the variety pack can be a good buy because you get several varieties without buying more than you can use. Larger families will save by slicing their own cold cuts. Differences in price between sliced and unsliced may be 15 cents or more per pound.

If you're buying hot dogs, read the label. If it says *all meat,* they are made of all meat products, usually beef, pork, and added seasonings. No fillers are permitted, and the maximum fat content is 30 percent.

If the label simply says *frankfurter, wiener,* or *hot dog,* it is made of a combination of meats, seasonings, and approved fillers, such as milk powder and soy flour. Again, it has a maximum fat content of 30 percent.

An *all beef* label indicates exclusive use of beef, with no other meats or fillers. The *kosher* label is used on some *all beef* products to show they have been produced under rabbinical supervision. Generally, there is garlic seasoning. Maximum fat content is 30 percent.

In deciding how much sausage to buy, consider these guidelines: for sandwiches, allow a pound of luncheon meat for eight sandwiches; adults and teenagers usually eat two frankfurters per person; a pound of pork sausage usually makes three or four servings when served with eggs or other foods; three or four kinds of cold meats make an attractive platter. For the mild-flavor cold meat varieties, allow six to eight servings per pound, and for stronger-flavored salami or cervelat, eight to twelve servings.

Here are the most popular sausages:

Ready-to-serve Varieties

Bologna. May be made of cured beef and pork or all beef. Second only to the frankfurter in popularity, the most common kinds are large and ring bologna. Buy them by the piece to slice or buy already sliced.

Cervelat (summer sausage). Made of beef and pork, mildly seasoned, then smoked or dried. It has no garlic. Popular varieties are *Farmer* and *Holsteiner.*

Head cheese. Actually not a cheese at all, but a chopped, cooked pork in a gelatin base. *Souse* is similar except for a sweet-sour flavor added by vinegar pickle.

Liver cheese (liver loaf). Simply sandwich-shaped slices of liver sausage, formed in a loaf shape, then covered with fresh white pork fat to keep it moist.

Liver sausage (liverwurst). Made of cooked liver and pork, seasoned with onions and spices. If it is smoked after cooking or has smoked meat, such as bacon, added, it's known as *Braunschweiger.*

Luncheon meat. Made of chopped ham, pork, and/or beef, tastily seasoned and ready to serve. It comes in round or square loaves, canned, in vacuum packages, or sliced.

Salami. Comes in two varieties—*soft* (or cooked) and *hard.* Soft salami is made from cured beef and pork which is cooked, then air dried for a short time. Two popular versions are *beer* salami and *cotto.* Soft salamis must be refrigerated, unlike the hard types which have been air dried from one to six months to remove 35 to 40 percent of the moisture. Most are highly seasoned with garlic, and some are smoked. *Pepperoni* and *genoa* are examples of dry salami.

Thuringer. Actually another type of cervelat, with a distinctive tangy flavor made of beef and ham or pork fat.

Heat or Cook-before-eating Varieties

Bockwurst. Light gray links made from veal and some pork. Milk, chives, eggs, and chopped parsley are added with seasonings similar to those used in frankfurters.

Bratwurst. Made from pork or a blend of pork and veal and highly seasoned. They come in chubby links slightly smaller than frankfurters. Bratwurst is available both fresh and fully cooked.

Fresh pork sausage. Made from ground pork, seasoned with pepper, sugar, sage, and salt. It is highly perishable and should be refrigerated immediately and cooked thoroughly before eating. It is sold in bulk, patties, rolls, and links, or in "brown and serve" links.

Country style fresh pork sausage. Principal differences between this and fresh pork sausage are in the grinding (somewhat coarser) and packaging (a long rope).

Smoked sausage. Made from cured beef and pork, then smoked to give a characteristic flavor and color. Varieties include *country-style* smoked sausage and *mettwurst.*

Knackwurst. Has ingredients similar to frankfurters and bolognas, with garlic added for stronger flavor. Made in wide natural casings or in skinless styles, they look like plump hot dogs. Although already fully cooked, knackwurst is usually served hot.

Polish sausage. Coarsely ground lean pork with beef added and highly seasoned with garlic. It is often referred to as *Kilbasa* which was originally a Polish word for sausage.

Chicken

During the Great Depression of the 1930s, a popular political promise was a "chicken in every pot," because in those days poultry was reserved for special Sunday and holiday dinners. Today we look to chicken and turkey as everyday sources of low-cost protein.

Almost all poultry you'll find in stores has been federally inspected and is Grade A, which means the birds are fully fleshed and meaty and attractive in appearance.

The age of the bird is the determining factor in tenderness. If the poultry is not young, the label will carry the word *mature,* or *old,* or similar words to identify its age. Common labeling terms are:

> YOUNG CHICKENS: young chicken, Rock Cornish game hen, broiler, fryer, roaster, or capon.
>
> YOUNG TURKEYS: young turkey, fryer-roaster, young hen, or young tom.
>
> YOUNG DUCKS: duckling, young duckling, broiler duckling, fryer duckling, or roaster duckling.
>
> MATURE CHICKENS: mature chicken, old chicken, hen, stewing chicken, or fowl.
>
> MATURE TURKEYS: mature turkey, yearling turkey, or old turkey.
>
> MATURE DUCKS, GEESE, AND GUINEAS: mature or old.

Mature birds are preferred for stewing, baking, soups, or salads, but you probably won't want them for roasting, frying, or broiling because they are less tender.

Poultry is perishable and demands handling and cooking with care. Use fresh-killed poultry within one to two days. If you don't plan to use it quickly, freeze it and keep it hard frozen. After thawing, cook it promptly. *Always* cook poultry completely at one time—*never* partially cook, store, and finish cooking at a later date. *Always* wash your hands after handling poultry to avoid contaminating other foods. If you're cutting up the poultry yourself, as is suggested for economy, be sure to clean thoroughly knives and cutting boards which have contacted the raw poultry before using them again. Avoid using wood cutting boards if you can. Also, be sure to remove the stuffing from the bird after serving and before you store any leftovers.

As reasonable in cost as chickens are throughout the year, people with freezer space look forward to stocking up when there's a sale. If you can learn, or persuade your husband to learn, how to cut up chickens, you'll save even more. Meat cutters are among the most highly paid employees in a supermarket, so the store can afford to sell whole chickens more cheaply than cut-up chickens. You can save enough to more than pay for your labor.

Here are some sample calculations, based on prices for chickens that were sale priced at 29 cents a pound. Four birds weighing a total of 12.27 pounds were purchased for a total cost of $3.56. After cutting, the four yielded the following quantities of cut-up parts:

Yield	Cost, if bought as parts
2 pounds, 14 ounces of breasts	$2.28
1 pound, 15 ounces of thighs	1.54
1 pound, 13 ounces of drumsticks	1.29
12 ounces of wing "drumsticks"	.36
3½ ounces chicken livers	.17
4 pounds, 8 ounces wings, necks, backs, and gizzards	
	$5.64

This total saving of more than $2.00 for less than a half hour's cutting time does not include the value of the four and a half pounds of backs, necks, and other parts which can be frozen for later cooking or put into a pot immediately to stew for soup or a casserole. Note that the above list includes cutting off the first joint of the wing to make wing "drumsticks," a favorite with small children. If you can learn to cut up chicken, you'll find the next step, boning the breasts, not so difficult. Boned chicken breasts can be an inexpensive and elegant meal for your next dinner party.

Instructions on how to cut up a whole chicken are given below.

How to Cut Up a Whole Chicken *

1. Begin by cutting off legs. Cut skin between thighs and body of chicken.

2. Lift chicken and bend back legs, grasping one leg with each hand. Bend legs until hip joints are loose.

3. Remove leg from body by cutting from back to front as close as possible to the back bone.

4. Then separate thigh and drumstick. Locate joint by squeezing between thigh and drumstick. Cut through joint.

5. To remove wing from body, start cutting on inside of wing just over the joint. Cut down and around the joint. To make the wing lie flat, make a small cut on the inside of the large wing joint. Cut just deep enough to expose the bones. Repeat with wing on other side.

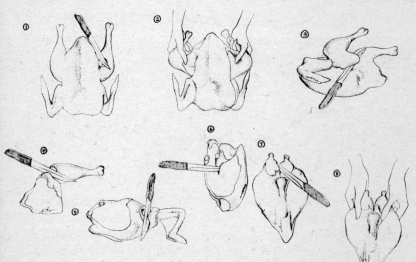

* source: National Broiler Council, Washington, D.C., 1972.

6. To cut the body into breast and back sections, place the chicken on neck end and cut from the tail along each side of back bone through rib joints to neck. Cut through the skin that attaches the neck-and-back strip to the breast. Place neck-and-back strip skin side up on cutting board. Cut into two pieces just above the spoon-shaped bones in the back.

Another method is to separate the back from the breast by cutting between the breast and back ribs from the shoulder to the tail end. Bend the back away from breast to separate the shoulder joints.

7. Place breast skin side down on cutting board. Cut through white cartilage at the V of the neck.

8. Hold breast firmly with both hands and bend back both sides. Push up with fingers to snap out the breastbone. Cut breast in half lengthwise.

Other Types of Poultry

The sheer abundance of broiler-fryers makes it all too easy to overlook other types of poultry.

Duckling. Often labeled *Long Island duckling,* it is generally sold quick frozen in weights ranging from 4 to 6 pounds. Figure on 4 servings per duckling because the usual practice is to cut them into quarters with poultry shears after roasting.

Capon. A young desexed male chicken, it has exceptional tenderness and flavor and a large amount of white meat. Weights range from 6 to 8 pounds.

Roasting chickens. A little older and larger than broiler-fryers, and weights range from 3½ to 6 pounds.

Rock Cornish game hens. A cross between a Cornish chicken and another breed, they range in weight from one pound up to a maximum of 2 pounds. The word *hen* does not imply female. Figure on 1 pound per serving.

Too many people still relegate turkey to Thanksgiving and Christmas dinners, but it deserves attention throughout the year.

In buying turkey the main rule to remember is the bigger the bird, the more meat for your money. Not only do the larger birds usually sell for a few cents less per pound, but they also have a larger proportion of meat to bone, so you get a bargain two ways.

Unfortunately, few home freezers have room to store a turkey of any size, so you'll need to roast it the week you buy it. Remember to allow enough time for a frozen turkey to defrost. The preferred method is refrigerator defrosting, which takes two to three days. An optional method is to put the turkey in its airtight wrapper in cold water for six to eight hours. A newer optional method is to leave the bird in its wrapper and place it in a closed, double-layer kraft bag of the type in which groceries are packed at the check-out counter. Allow about 12 hours defrosting time for birds under 12 pounds; larger birds, up to 25 pounds, will be ready for roasting in about 16 hours.

Never buy a turkey in a leaky bag. If you see one, notify the meat manager.

The handling rule we mentioned with chicken applies to turkey—handle with care.

If you don't have a freezer, choose a smaller turkey or turkey parts, which are available in most markets today. Turkey parts are also the answer for the family who prefers only white or only dark meat. It is possible to select breast, drumstick, wing, or boned roasts which offer white meat, dark meat, or a combination of both. Because some of the waste associated with a whole turkey is eliminated, you can afford to pay more for turkey by the part. For example, according to U.S. Department of Agriculture figures, if a whole turkey is priced at 59 cents a pound, you can afford to pay the following prices for turkey parts and still get equal value for your dollar.

Part	Cost which is equal value to whole turkey at 59 cents a pound
Turkey breast	$0.75
Drumstick	0.60
Wing	0.55
Boned roast	
White and dark meat	1.03

| White meat | 1.03 |
| Dark meat | 1.03 |

Self-basting turkeys are relatively new on the market. They are priced higher than regular turkeys, but for many people the juicier quality of the cooked meat makes up for the additional cost. The label will tell you whether the basting solution is straight butter, plain broth, or mixtures of oil and water in various proportions.

Ground turkey is found in some markets and can be used in recipes calling for ground beef. Be sure the ground turkey is cooked thoroughly.

Seafood—Fresh, Frozen, or by the Can

If you're lucky enough to live in a section of the country that is relatively near a source of fresh fish or shellfish, your supermarket may have a fresh seafood service counter. Check it every week because it may offer bargains in fresh fish.

If you do buy fresh fish, serve it as soon as possible, preferably the same day. Fish should be eaten soon after it is caught so that the delicate flavor is not lost.

Look for fish with bright, clear eyes, which may protrude a little. As fish stales, the eyes turn cloudy and sunken. Gills should be red and free from slime, and the skin should be shiny, with color unfaded.

Freezing fresh fish is not generally recommended, mainly because the fresh-caught flavor is lost and because the commercially frozen product is good and reasonably priced.

Fish Fillets

These are the most convenient form of fish, whether fresh or frozen, and best for those who have small children or who don't want to bother with bones. Fillets are the sides of fish, cut lengthwise away from the backbone. They have few, if any, bones and may be skinless as well. Fillets can be cooked in a variety of ways.

Steaks are cross-section slices from large dressed fish, 5/8 inch to 1 inch thick. A cross section of the backbone is the only bone in the steak. As with beef steak, these are most often broiled with butter.

For convenience, you also can buy frozen breaded fish portions or sticks. These may be either raw or already fried. Government regulations require that raw portions must weigh 1½ ounces and be at least ⅜ inch thick and contain not less than 65 percent fish. Precooked fish sticks have the same size and weight requirements but are required to contain 60 percent or more fish.

Canned Fish and Seafood

Tuna. Packed from six species—*albacore, blackfin, bluefin, skipjack, yellowfin,* and *little* tuna. Albacore has lighter meat than the others and is the only one permitted to be labeled *white meat* tuna. The others are labeled *light meat.* Canned tuna is packed in oil or water. In descending order of price, the packs of tuna are solid, chunk, and flaked or grated. It is convenient to have several kinds on hand; solid-pack, white meat can be used for a showy salad plate, and chunk or flaked, light meat can be used for tuna salad sandwiches or for a casserole, in which flavor and protein value rather than the size of the pieces, are important.

Salmon. Packed from five species. Most expensive is *sockeye* or *red.* Then in descending order of price are *chinook* or *king, medium red, silver* or *coho, pink,* and last, *chum* or *keta.* Highest priced varieties are a deep red in color and have a high oil content. Again, you may want to stock two or three varieties and use red salmon for salads, chinook, king, or coho for sandwiches, and chum or keta for fish cakes, where color is less important.

Canned sardines. Good in hors d'oeuvres and sandwiches, they come from Maine and the Pacific and are imported from Norway and Portugal (*brisling* or *sprat*). Pacific sardines are larger than Maine sardines and usually are packed in tomato sauce. Maine sardines are packed in vegetable oil, tomato sauce, or mustard sauce.

The amount of fish to buy per serving varies with the recipe to be used and the size of the appetite. Generally speaking, allow 3 ounces per serving of cooked boneless fish, which means buying about ½ pound per serving in dressed or pan-dressed fish, and about ⅙ pound per serving for canned fish because of the concentration of meat in the can.

CHAPTER 3

The Dairy Department

The admonition to "drink your milk" springs so naturally to most mothers' lips they hardly know they're saying it. They know how valuable milk is. Milk is the main food source of calcium and an excellent source of protein and riboflavin, a B vitamin. It is not only essential to children's growth but necessary to body maintenance throughout life.

Unfortunately, teenage girls—whom statistics show to be the most undernourished group in our country—are the most likely to skip milk, just at the time when they should be drinking four or more glasses a day. Adults, although they require just two glasses a day, often tend not to drink any milk on the theory that they no longer need it and because they'd rather get their nutrients elsewhere.

Getting Milk into the Diet

Of course, the easiest way to get the day's supply of milk into the diet is to serve it as a beverage or to serve some of the products made with milk, such as ice cream and cheese. But you can use milk in preparing main dishes, cream soups, puddings, and other foods. There is about as much calcium in each of the following amounts of milk products and milk-rich foods as there is in 1 cup of fresh whole milk:

> 1⅓ ounces natural cheddar cheese
> 1½ ounces processed cheddar cheese
> 1⅓ cups creamed cottage cheese
> 1 ounce Swiss cheese
> 1 cup custard
> 1⅓ cups ice cream
> 1 cup ice milk
> ¾ cup homemade macaroni and cheese
> ⅕ of 14-inch round pizza, made with cheese topping
> 1 cup pudding, made with milk and cornstarch
> 1⅓ cups canned cream soup, prepared with equal amount milk
> 1 cup yogurt

Obviously, some of the milk-rich soups and puddings may be prepared with nonfat instant milk or evaporated milk rather than regular fluid milk, and this is one way you can save on costs.

Some Comparisons of Milk Costs

Milk prices vary throughout the country because they're established by federal milk marketing orders, which are based on regional supply and cost differences. However, in a given city the relationships of the prices of various milk products will stay the same. The following prices, collected in the Washington, D.C. area in May 1972, offer a relative basis for comparison.

Homogenized Vitamin D Milk	Price
1 gallon carton	$1.21 (30¢ a quart)
½ gallon carton	.61 (30.5¢ a quart)
1 quart	.35
Skim milk, fortified with A and D	
½ gallon	.59
1 quart	.32
Instant nonfat dry milk, fortified	
1 quart (reconstituted)	.15
Evaporated milk	
1 quart (reconstituted)	.19
Combination of half reconstituted nonfat dry milk and regular whole milk	.23

If you can use them, the half-gallon cartons of fluid milk are a substantial saving. Using nonfat dry milk, of course, offers the greatest possibility for saving costs.

Mixing equal parts of regular milk with reconstituted nonfat dry milk for drinking purposes yields a product that many people find hard to distinguish from whole milk. Always make sure it's served very cold. To cook with nonfat dry milk, just mix the powder with the dry ingredients called for in your recipe and add water equal to the amount specified for milk.

Choosing from the Different Types of Milk

Remember that you're buying milk primarily for its protein and calcium values, which will remain, no matter what its form. If you're economizing or reducing calories by buying some low fat, nonfortified products, be sure you're getting sufficient vitamins A and D elsewhere. Consult the daily food guide in the appendix for alternatives. Here are some guidelines for milk and milk products that may help you to weigh one value against another.

Milk. Almost all fresh whole pasteurized milk on the market today is homogenized, a process that disperses the fat evenly through the milk. Vitamin D fortification is also almost a universal practice. There are 160 calories per 8-ounce glass.

Skim milk (nonfat milk). Fluid skimmed milk has all the nutrients of whole milk, except fat, which is reduced to 0.5 percent, and vitamins A and D. Skimmed milk frequently is fortified to replace vitamins A and D, and some have added nonfat dry milk solids; check the label. An 8-ounce glass contains 90 calories.

Two-percent milk. Made from fresh whole and skimmed milk, this has only 2 percent milk fat, as compared to the 3.25 percent in whole milk. It, too, is often fortified to be comparable to fortified whole milk. There are 150 calories per 8-ounce glass.

Nonfat dry milk. Nonfat dry milk is made by removing fat and water from pasteurized fluid milk. It is usually sold in an instant form. Most of the protein, minerals, and vitamins of the fluid milk are retained, and it may be fortified with vitamins A and D. It has the advantages of needing no refrigeration in dry form, of easy storage to assure adequate supply, and of mixing and measuring easily. When reconstituted, it is comparable to skim milk and has 90 calories per 8-ounce glass.

Evaporated milk. It may be made from either fresh whole milk or skim milk and concentrated to remove about 60 percent of the water. It is usually fortified with vitamin D. When mixed with an equal volume of water, it is about the same in nutritive value and calories as the milk from which it was made, either 160 calories or 90 calories per 8-ounce glass.

Sweetened condensed milk. This is made from fresh whole milk, with about half the water removed, and contains about 40 percent sugar. If not diluted with water, it has 982 calories per 8 ounces.

Chocolate milk, chocolate-flavored milk, and chocolate drink. Chocolate milk is made from whole milk with chocolate and sweetener added; it has 210 calories per glass. Chocolate-flavored milk is made from whole milk with cocoa and sweetener; it also has 210 calories per glass. Chocolate drink is made from skim or low-fat milk with chocolate and sweetener, and nonfat milk solids may be added; it has 190 calories per glass. There also is a chocolate-flavored drink which is made from skim or lowfat milk with cocoa added; it, too, has 190 calories per glass.

Buttermilk. Cultured buttermilk is made by adding lactic-acid producing bacteria to fresh pasteurized skim milk. It is much thicker than skim milk but has similar nutritive value and calories. Usually it has about 1 percent fat with 90 to 112 calories per 8-ounce glass. If butter granules are added, calorie count and vitamin A content tend to increase somewhat.

Yogurt. Yogurt has a mildly tangy flavor and is usually made by combining skim or partially skimmed milk with a bacterial culture. One cup of plain yogurt contains 120 calories. If it is fruit flavored, it may contain as many as 250 calories.

Cultured sour cream. As its name implies, it is made from fresh pasteurized sweet cream and usually has about 18 percent fat. A tablespoon has 30 calories.

Sweet cream. Table cream (coffee cream or light cream) is at least 18 percent milk fat and is generally homogenized. Light whipping cream has at least 30 percent milk fat, and heavy whipping cream has from 36 percent to 40 percent milk fat. The range of calories per tablespoon is 30 calories for coffee cream and 45 to 55 for whipping cream.

Half and half. This is a mixture of milk and cream. In some markets sour half and half is available. With 11 percent milk fat, 1 tablespoon equals 20 calories.

Cottage cheese. Made from skimmed milk, plain cottage cheese has practically no fat. Creamed cottage cheese, which has sweet cream added, has a higher calorie count but gains additional nutritive value from the cream fat. Many dieters seem to operate on the theory that any kind of cottage cheese is low in calories, but as the figures show, buy the plain kind if calories count; there are 100 calories per half-cup of plain cottage cheese and 120 calories per half-cup of the creamed variety.

Whipped Cream and Whipped Toppings

If your menu calls for whipped cream, consider a number of comparable products that differ in cost, calories, and convenience.

First, there's regular whipping cream, which in Washington, D.C. in July 1972 was priced at 43 cents per 8 ounces or, because it doubles in volume when whipped, enough to make 2 cups.

Then there's evaporated milk. A 13-ounce can costs 18 to 20 cents, and half a can, when chilled in the freezer first and then beaten, will triple in volume. This then gives you more than 2 cups of whipped product for about 9 cents, and fewer calories, too.

And, there's nonfat dry milk, which is simple to combine with the ice water and beat into stiff peaks. Result, 2 cups of even lower-calorie whipped topping for only about 5 cents.

If you don't want to whip the cream yourself, you can buy pressurized whipped toppings in aerosol cans at prices ranging from 49 cents to 57 cents for 9 ounces. If push-button convenience is important to you, the extra price may be worth it. There are two basic kinds of toppings—a dairy product made from milk solids, flavoring, and sugar with cream; and a nondairy type which has a vegetable oil base and no milk or cream.

There are also frozen toppings, at prices ranging from 33 cents for 4½ ounces to 59 cents for 6¾ ounces. The higher price is for a squeeze container with decorator tip; again you're paying extra for the ease of use. The advantage of frozen and pressurized toppings is that they can be kept on hand for immediate use when you're in a hurry. Also, you can use a small quantity without the bother of whipping an entire batch.

Storing Milk Products

Fresh milk, cream, and other milk products should, of course, be refrigerated as soon as possible after purchase. Milk left standing in the sunlight will lose its riboflavin content and may also lose in flavor.

Unopened cans of evaporated and sweet condensed milk may be kept at room temperature or in a cool place, as may unopened packages of nonfat dry milk. After opening, these types of milk products should be refrigerated and tightly covered. The evaporated and condensed milk, once opened, should be used within five days; the dry milk will keep a few weeks.

Ice Cream and Frozen Desserts

Ice cream is a dessert enjoyed by almost everyone. It is nutritious, too. Remember that 1⅓ cups of ice cream or 1 cup of soft ice milk will give children as much calcium as 1 glass of milk.

Most stores offer ice cream in a wide range of sizes, from single servings to pint, quart, half-gallon, and gallon containers. If your family size, ice cream appetite, and freezer space justify it, the larger sizes will be your best buy.

Ice cream is frozen either hard or soft. The popular, fairly hard, ice cream is made from cream, milk, sugar, and stabilizers and contains at least 10 percent milkfat and 20 percent total milk solids. Softer ice cream is known as frozen custard and French or French custard ice cream. This creamy dessert is made from the same ingredients used for ice cream but at least 1.4 percent egg yolk solids are added, which gives you added vitamin A. Often ingredients such as chocolate syrup, fruits, nuts, or confectioner's sugar are added to the basic mix, in which case the requirements for milk fat and total milk solids are reduced to 8 and 16 percent.

The major price differences between ice creams are usually between regular and "premium" types. The premium or rich ice creams have more milk fat, generally use higher quality ingredients, and have less air, so they command a higher price and may well be worth it to you.

Ice milk has less milk fats and total milk solids than does ice cream, but it is likely to have more sugar and incorporate less air. Although it would seem that ice milk has fewer calories, the calorie count of ice milk and ice cream are almost the same when equal volumes are compared. Any artificial flavoring must be indicated on the label for ice milk.

Fruit sherbets have a pleasing tart flavor from added fruits or fruit juices and contain 1 to 2 percent milk fat and 2 to 5 percent total milk solids. However, because of the method of making sherbets, the calorie content of one cup of sherbet is not as much below that of ice cream and ice milk as might be expected from the low fat content of sherbet.

Ice cream may be stored in the freezing compartment of a combination refrigerator-freezer model for two to three weeks. Place an entire carton in the freezer. Once the carton has been opened, press a piece of foil or transparent plastic wrap over the exposed surface. Covering the exposed surface will protect the ice cream from absorbing refrigerator odors and will prevent the development of a tough leathery discolored skin that is caused by evaporation from the surface layer.

Ice cream should not be allowed to partially melt and then be rehardened. This causes the ice crystals to increase in size, which results in a coarse, icy body.

Butter and Margarine

Everybody knows of the difference in cost between butter and margarine. However, there's also a substantial differential between whipped butter and regular butter and between margarine in sticks and soft margarine in little tubs. If you like the flavor and texture of whipped butter or the spreadability of soft margarine, you may want to pay the price. To help make your selection, it may be helpful to quickly review each product.

Butter

By law, butter must contain not less than 80 percent milk fat. It may or may not contain salt. If no salt is added, it is labeled *unsalted* or *sweet*. The highest quality butter is made from sweet cream or sometimes from sweet cream with a culture added to it, very much like the culture that is used in making buttermilk.

Whipped butter is made by forcing air or an inert gas into butter, which increases the volume and also makes it easier to spread.

Most of the butter you see in your supermarket has the USDA shield with a letter grade indicating the butter's quality. *U.S. Grade AA* butter is made from high-quality, fresh sweet cream. It has a delicate flavor, with a fine, highly pleasing aroma and smooth texture with good spreadability. Butter graded *U.S. Grade A* also has pleasing flavor and aroma but is not quite as fine as the top grade. *U.S. Grade B*, sold only in a few areas, may have a slightly acid flavor and is generally made from selected sour cream. This flavor is actually preferred by some people who use it as a spread or in cooking or baking.

Fresh butter has a very delicate flavor of its own but is quick to pick up other odors. To maintain its delicate flavor, store butter in the original wrappings until ready for use. Keep it in the coldest part of the refrigerator and only remove as much as you will use at one time.

Margarine, the Economical Spread

Oleomargarine has come a long way from the days when it looked like lard and you had to work a little bead of yellow dye through it. Today it is flavorful, vitamin-enriched, and available in several varieties. One thing hasn't changed though—it's still economical. It averages about one-third of the cost of butter.

Margarine, like butter, must contain 80 percent fat. The main ingredient is usually vegetable oil, although animal fat is sometimes added. There is also a small percentage of carefully cultured skim milk, usually some salt, except for those marked *unsalted*, and government-regulated amounts of vitamin A and, sometimes, vitamin D. If you're concerned about cholesterol, you many want to use the margarines made with corn oil. Because they are a specialty item, they cost a few cents more.

Conventional or regular margarine is cheapest. It is the type that comes in sticks, like regular butter. The oils and fats in these margarines have been slightly hardened during processing so that they approach the consistency of butter. Even so, margarine is slightly more spreadable than butter.

A newer variety that costs a little more is soft margarine. It is usually sold in plastic containers ready for the table and is very spreadable.

Margarine can be used for any purpose, from table to cooking, for which butter would ordinarily be used but with one exception: butter heated in a pan will "brown," whereas margarine tends to scorch if you aren't careful. If you add a small amount of vegetable oil to the pan, scorching will be prevented.

Eggs

In addition to being highly valued as a source of protein, eggs provide fat, an excellent supply of vitamins A and D, iron, and riboflavin.

In considering good buys in eggs, it is helpful to know how to figure the cost per serving—which, as you remember, was emphasized in the discussion of meats in Chapter 2. If eggs are 60 cents per dozen, for example, a serving of 2 eggs costs only 10 cents. Nutritionists say that in buying a dozen large eggs at 60 cents the shopper is paying 40 cents a pound for high quality protein; eggs are a bargain.

Common market sizes of eggs per dozen are:

Extra Large	27 ounces
Large	24 ounces
Medium	21 ounces
Small	18 ounces

First of all, you will want to select the size that fits your needs. Recipes tend to be based on large or medium eggs. Actually, substitution of one egg size for another makes little difference in most recipes; the exceptions are recipes, such as sponge or angelfood cakes, in which the proportion of eggs is important. If there is less than a 7 or 8 cent difference in the price per dozen between two sizes of eggs of the same grade, the larger size is the better buy per pound. If the difference is greater than 7 or 8 cents, the smaller size is the better buy.

Most supermarkets carry both AA and A grade eggs, and sometimes Grade B eggs are available. Grade is an index of quality, particularly of how high the yolk stands and how compact the white is. Grade B eggs are perfectly satisfactory if you plan to use them relatively soon, but you may wish to pay the modest premium for the higher quality.

In New England many people have a traditional preference for brown shell eggs, and stores tend to carry them. The shell color hasn't the slightest effect on the nutritional value or quality of the egg.

Eggs tend to be most plentiful, and thus lower in price, during the winter and more expensive in the summertime when hot weather tends to slow down the egg laying cycle. So, wintertime is often a time when you should think of budget-balancing main dishes made from eggs, such as soufflés, omelets, or egg foo yung, which is a great way to make a "planned-over" out of leftover meat.

Almost everyone regularly faces the problem of the leftover yolks or whites. They can be refrigerated and used later if you follow these procedures: place yolks in a jar, add just enough water to cover, and chill; use within two or three days. Keep whites chilled in a covered jar; they will keep from seven to ten days.

Cheese—An Original Convenience Food

Because cheese is made from milk, it becomes a concentrated source of most of the nutrients in milk, especially protein and minerals. As well as being exotic and delicious, it is highly nutritious.

One reason cheese is available in such a wide range of varieties is that it is made from different kinds of milk. Most American cheese is made from cow's milk; Scandinavia uses a lot of goat's milk; and France makes some cheeses from sheep's milk. The hardest or firmest cheeses are the lowest in moisture content and require long periods of ripening, which produces the particular sharp flavor. These cheeses can be stored a year or more under favorable conditions. Softer cheese has more moisture and is correspondingly more perishable.

All cheese that you find in the refrigerated dairy case should, of course, be put in the refrigerator when you get home. Some of the cheese products that are on the nonrefrigerated shelves may be left out, but only until they are opened. They, too, must be refrigerated after opening.

To prevent cheese from drying out, store it in an airtight container. Many cheeses are given a wax coating, a perfect insulator, before they are sold. However, when you start to use them, you necessarily break the seal, so these cheeses must be wrapped tightly before returning to the refrigerator. Unsliced cheese usually keeps longer than sliced cheese because air can't get to it as easily. Mold sometimes develops on cheese when it is stored for a long period. This mold is harmless but should be cut off before using the cheese.

Basic Types of Cheese

There are two basic types of cheese—natural and processed. Natural cheese is made from milk which is coagulated. The solid part, or curd, is separated from the watery part, or whey. Cold pack or club cheese is natural cheese that has been ground or blended to make it softer and more spreadable. There are many varieties of natural cheese. The glossary at the end of this chapter will help you identify them.

Pasteurized process cheese is made by grinding and mixing natural cheeses and then heating and stirring them together. The result is an entirely different product. An emulsifying agent is added as well as small amounts of liquid, salt, acid, color, and flavorings to further change the texture and flavor. Sometimes fruits, vegetables, or meats are added.

Processed cheeses have a milder flavor and softer body than the natural cheeses from which they were made. Also, they keep better because pasteurizing stops the curing. Processed cheeses are good to use in cooking because they melt easily and blend well with other foods. For the same reason, they are the usual choice for toasted cheese sandwiches or cheeseburgers. There is no rind so there is no waste.

Process cheese food also is a blend of cheeses that have been pasteurized. It may be plain or have ingredients added. However, it contains less cheese and fat and more milk or whey solids and water. It is milder in flavor and softer in texture and therefore spreads and melts more easily than regular cheese.

Process cheese spread is much the same as cheese food except it has even more moisture and less milk fat, and a stabilizer usually is added to prevent separation of the ingredients. It is an extremely soft and spreadable processed cheese.

Variety in Cheese Prices

The enormous variety in blends of cheese and in varieties of natural cheese is reflected in the prices. Understanding why the prices are different and then relating them to the use you want to make of the cheese can pay dividends in your food budget.

Most expensive, of course, are the imported cheeses. Many people find a domestic blue cheese perfectly satisfactory for salad dressing and willingly pass up a more expensive imported Roquefort.

The amount of aging is also a factor in the price of cheese. You'll be particularly aware of this with cheddar if you're a lover of extra sharp cheese. The longer it's been aged, the sharper it becomes, and because aging is expensive, you may find an extra sharp cheddar costing 20 cents a pound more than the mild variety.

Many families buy processed cheeses without realizing the differences between them. Of three different types, the processed cheese spread is the least expensive because it has the most moisture. Processed cheese food is more expensive, and plain processed cheese is the highest priced because it has the least moisture.

The range of prices of cheese is illustrated by the following sample made in Washington, D.C., in July 1972:

Cheese	Price Per Pound
Extra sharp cheddar	$1.19
Sharp cheddar	1.13
Mild cheddar	0.99
Processed cheese	0.95
Processed cheese food	0.90
Processed cheese spread	0.70

As you can see, on a straight per pound basis, the lowest price is for processed cheese spread which you can slice yourself. One reason it is lower priced is because it has more moisture; this also makes it a good product for recipes that call for melted cheese. But remember, too, that processed cheese has a greater nutritional value than cheese food and cheese spread.

You may sometimes prefer the convenience of presliced cheese or of individually wrapped slices. Also, you may like to keep grated cheeses on hand for sprinkling over spaghetti or on top of casseroles. For such convenience you will, of course, pay extra.

No matter how carefully you store cheese, you may find yourself with some pieces of dried-out cheese. Keep a container on hand in the refrigerator in which to grate any dried pieces of cheese. Don't worry about mixing cheddar with blue and mozzarella—the more, the merrier. The combination of flavors really produces very interesting results when sprinkled into an omelet, on top of a casserole, or on a salad.

A Brief Glossary of Cheeses

Bel Paese. Mild, with a smooth body, slightly gray on the outside and creamy yellow inside; used as dessert, on crackers, and in sandwiches.

Blue (and Bleu). A spicy, semisoft, crumbly white cheese with veins of blue-green mold; used as dessert, in dips, cooked foods, and salads and salad dressings.

Brick. A milk, light yellow to orange, brick-shaped cheese, with a semisoft texture; used in sandwiches and salads.

Brie. May vary from mild to pungent, has a thin white crust with a creamy yellow interior; used either as an appetizer or dessert.

Caciocavallo. A solid, sharp cheese, light tan on the outside, with a light interior, comes in a tenpin shape and is used grated for seasoning; similar to provolone, but not smoked.

Camembert. Can vary from mild to sharp, comes in wedges with a thin crust and yellow interior; used mostly as an elegant dessert; sometimes canned and, once opened, spoils rather quickly.

Cheddar. Ranges from mild to sharp (there's often an indication on the package), has a light yellow or orange color, a hard, firm body appearing in many shapes; used in sandwiches and cooked foods.

Colby. Mild, hard cheese, yellow or orange in color, though softer than cheddar; used in sandwiches and cooked foods.

Cream. Mild, slightly acid, soft and smooth, white in color, packaged in rectangular foil-wrapped portions, or in plastic cartons; used in sandwiches, salads, spread on crackers, and in desserts.

Edam. Hard, though softer than cheddar, creamy yellow, comes in a cannonball shape encased with red wax, has a mild flavor; used on crackers and with fruit.

Gjetost. A round, golden brown, hard cheese, with a caramel flavor; used on crackers.

Gorgonzola. Spicy, semisoft cheese, streaked with blue-green mold, as in blue cheese, is round in shape; used as dessert.

Gouda. Mild, hard cheese, round in shape, with a yellow color, sometimes wrapped in red wax; used on crackers and with fruit.

Gruyere. A hard, somewhat sweet cheese, with tiny holes, has a light yellow color; used as dessert; natural gruyere is very similar to Swiss cheese.

Liederkranz. Soft, smooth, creamy yellow cheese, with a strong flavor; used as appetizer, dessert, as a snack.

Limburger. Soft, smooth, creamy white cheese, quite strong in flavor; used on sandwiches and crackers.

Monterey (Jack). Mild, semisoft, creamy white cheese; used mostly in sandwiches.

Mozzarella. Semisoft, creamy white, pliable cheese, mild in flavor; is used in pizza and other cooked foods.

Muenster. Has smooth, waxy texture and a mellow flavor, with a yellow, tan or white exterior and white interior; used in sandwiches.

Neufchatel. Mildly flavored, creamy white cheese, wrapped in rectangular portions; used in sandwiches, dips, and salads; similar to cream cheese, but lower in fat.

Parmesan. Light yellow, brittle cheese, sharp in flavor; used grated as seasoning.

Port du Salut. Smooth, buttery cheese with a sharp flavor, brownish red on the outside, with a creamy yellow interior; used as dessert and with fruit.

Provolone. Firm, smooth, sharp cheese, usually smoked, which comes in sausage or salami shapes bound with cord; used in cooked foods; prepackaged provolone in wedges is popular for appetizers and sandwiches.

Ricotta. Soft, white cheese, which can be either moist or dry, with a bland, or somewhat sweet flavor, appearing in plastic or metal containers; used in cooked foods or as seasoning, when dry; in the moist form, it is highly perishable.

Romano. Sharp, very hard, granular cheese, light yellow in color; used as seasoning, grating and for general table use.

Roquefort. Semisoft, spicy white cheese, mixed with blue-green mold, and sometimes crumbly; used as dessert, in salads, and on crackers.

Stilton. White, semisoft, crumbly spicy cheese, mixed with blue-green mold; used as dessert and in cooked foods.

Swiss. Hard, smooth, sweetish, cheese with large holes, which comes in blocks or large wheels; used in sandwiches and salads.

CHAPTER 4

The Produce Department

There's probably no more exciting place in the supermarket than the produce counter. Here you really get to see, smell, and hold a product before making a selection.

Modern production, shipping, storage, and marketing methods make a great variety of fresh produce possible year round. We take it almost for granted that we can start a midwinter day with juice from Florida oranges, put bananas from Central America on our cereal, and have tomatoes from Texas and lettuce from Arizona in our luncheon sandwich. At dinnertime we enjoy a salad made of tangy apples from New York State, celery from Michigan, or cabbage and raisins from California and, of course, have a baked potato from Idaho or Maine and a dessert of fresh pears from Washington.

Take a look at your family's meals to see whether each member is getting the fresh fruits he needs for vitamin C and the dark green and deep yellow vegetables that are rich in vitamin A—to say nothing of the minerals and other nutrients found in these foods. Because vitamin C is not stored by the body, and we need it daily, it's especially important to see that meals include at least one serving a day of foods which are good sources of vitamin C or two servings of those which are considered fair sources. Citrus fruits, strawberries, and cantaloupes, sweet peppers, broccoli, and brussels sprouts are good sources of the vitamin C. Tomatoes, raw cabbage, potatoes, kale, and turnip greens are fair sources.

Yellow and green vegetables and fruits are great sources of Vitamin A. A general rule is that the greener the leaf, or the deeper yellow the flesh, the more vitamin A. This means that the darker green outside leaves of the head of iceberg lettuce are nutritionally more valuable than the inside leaves.

If you've been buying only the familiar fresh fruits and vegetables, you'll find the glossary at the end of this chapter very helpful. It tells you how to prepare the less common fruits and vegetables as well as the common ones and what to look for in selecting good quality.

Getting Values for Your Dollars in Produce

Fresh fruits and vegetables are usually best in quality and lowest in cost in peak season. The calendar of seasonal supplies offered here shows when you can expect to find the most plentiful supply of various fruits and vegetables in most parts of the country. Such produce as cabbage, carrots, onions, and potatoes are available all year and are not included in the chart.

Summertime is, of course, the best produce time, but if you're lucky enough to live in or near a growing area for any of the fruits and vegetables, you will undoubtedly find bargains at other times of the year, too. Remember that a freeze in Florida at a crucial time, or a drought in the Midwest, can affect the plentifuls listed for specific months. Sudden swings in supply due to weather conditions may have fairly sharp effects on prices, as, for example, when rain in the fields prevents picking, and prices shoot up almost overnight.

SEASONAL BUYING CALENDAR FOR FRUITS AND VEGETABLES

January	February	March	April	May	June
Brussels sprouts	Belgian endive	Artichokes	Artichokes	Artichokes	Apricots
Grapefruit	Broccoli	Asparagus	Asparagus	Asparagus	Asparagus
Oranges	Brussels sprouts	Belgian endive	Belgian endive	Grapefruit	Beans, snap
Parsnips	Grapefruit	Broccoli	Grapefruit	Pineapples	Beets
Tangelos	Oranges	Grapefruit	Green peas	Rhubarb	Blueberries
Tangerines	Rhubarb	Honeydews	Pineapples	Strawberries	Cantaloupes
Turnips;		Oranges	Rhubarb	Watermelons	Cherries
rutabagas		Pineapples	Strawberries		Corn, sweet
		Rhubarb			Cucumbers
					Honeydews
					Lemons
					Limes
					Okra
					Peaches
					Peas, green
					Plums; prunes
					Radishes
					Rhubarb
					Strawberries
					Tomatoes
					Watermelons

SEASONAL BUYING CALENDAR FOR FRUITS AND VEGETABLES (continued)

July	August	September	October	November	December
Apricots	Beets	Beets	Apples	Apples	Apples
Beans, snap	Blueberries	Eggplant	Brussels sprouts	Brussels sprouts	Brussels sprouts
Beets	Cantaloupes	Grapes	Cauliflower	Cauliflower	Cranberries
Blueberries	Corn, sweet	Honeydews	Cranberries	Cranberries	Endive
Cantaloupes	Eggplant	Okra	Grapes	Sweet potatoes	Sweet potatoes
Cherries	Grapes	Peaches	Parsnips	Tangelos	Tangelos
Corn, sweet	Honeydews	Pears	Pears	Tangerines	Tangerines
Cucumbers	Limes	Plums; prunes	Pumpkins	Turnips;	
Grapes	Okra		Sweet potatoes	rutabagas	
Lemons	Peaches		Turnips;		
Limes	Pears		rutabagas		
Okra	Plums; prunes				
Peaches	Tomatoes				
Plums; prunes	Watermelons				
Tomatoes					
Watermelons					

Using the Seasonal Specials

Keep an eye on this calendar, but remember to check the ads for seasonal buys. The produce counter is also the place in the store where you're most likely to find unadvertised good buys. If a store has overordered bananas, lettuce, brussels sprouts, or avocados, they need to sell them before they spoil. Buy them only if you can use them immediately. Don't get carried away by seasonal specials on such things as peaches and melons which are highly perishable. Bargains which end up in the garbage can are not bargains.

In addition to being alert to seasonal bargains, think about the use you're going to make of your purchases, particularly of fruits. Small apples, bananas, and oranges may be a better buy, even at a slightly higher price, if they're destined for children's snacks.

If you're planning to bake potatoes, you'll probably want good-sized ones, but don't overlook the possibility of little potatoes boiled in their jackets. Often they're cheaper because many people tend to buy the large ones.

The produce department is a great place to make use of the "splurge-a-little, save-a-little" concept. If your family particularly likes asparagus or fresh mushrooms and you find them a little out of your normal budget range, go ahead and enjoy them and economize by finding new ways to cook such old standbys as cabbage or celery. Braised celery or gently-cooked cabbage with a cheese sauce are not only low-cost in most seasons of the year, but a taste and nutrition treat. Investigate the pleasures of such old-fashioned vegetables as parsnips and turnips, or try an egg-plant-sausage casserole as an inexpensive main dish.

Making the Best of Produce

Remember that freshness is the key to the essential goodness of fruits and vegetables. Important nutrients can literally evaporate if you keep fruits and vegetables too long, which is why there is so much emphasis on prompt storage and use. The storage charts in the appendix should be helpful.

The other way to lose important vitamins and minerals is by overcooking vegetables in too much water. Almost every vegetable benefits from being cooked in only enough water to prevent scorching. Vitamin C is especially water soluble, and some of it ends up in the cooking liquid, so try to save water in which vegetables have been cooked to use in gravies, sauces, and soups. That way, you're preserving the vitamins you paid for.

Also keep in mind that the nutrients in fruits and vegetables tend to be stored close to the skin or peel, so serve or prepare them without peeling whenever possible. That's why we like to see people bake or boil potatoes in their jackets and encourage children to eat apples with the skin on them. If you must peel, try to make the peeling as thin as possible.

Fruits

In general, select fruit for the best eating quality. Attractive appearance is not always the indication of fine quality—there are other characteristics that help you to judge the degrees of ripeness and flavor. Whole citrus fruits, your best source of vitamin C, keep their nutrients well at room temperature, but berries are highly perishable and need careful handling to conserve their nutrients. Be a good customer—don't pinch and squeeze. Customers' rough handling of fruits causes spoilage and waste—and loss from careless handling gets passed along to you in higher prices.

Apples

There is an apple to suit almost every taste. Apples should be firm and have good color and no blemishes or soft spots.

Large quantities of apples can be stored in a cool, dark, airy place for several weeks. They should be sorted every once in a while and those that show any sign of spoilage should be removed so that the rest are not affected. Apples will keep for one or two weeks in the refrigerator if stored in plastic bags to prevent shriveling, or may be placed loose in the refrigerator hydrator.

Apples will turn brown very quickly when cut, but this can be prevented by sprinkling the slices with lemon or an acid fruit juice.

Some of the widely available types of apples include:

Delicious. Bright red, solid, striped skin; five points at blossom end; yellowish-white flesh; juicy and very mildly tart; used for eating. Season: September–April

Golden Delicious. Yellow or golden skin; yellowish-white flesh; juicy and sweet; used for eating and salads; will not darken as readily when cut. Season: October–April

Jonathan. Bright red skin; white or slightly yellow flesh; sometimes tinged with red; juicy and slightly tart; used for eating, pies. Season: September–February

McIntosh. Bright, deep red skin; striped with carmine; white flesh; juicy and slightly tart, becoming mild and nearly sweet when ripe; used for eating, sauce, pies, and baking. Season: October–February

Northern Spy. Bright red skin, stripes over yellow; yellowish flesh; very juicy; used for eating, sauce, pies, and baking. Season: October–March

Rome Beauty. Yellow skin mingled with red; white flesh with slight yellow or greenish tinge; juicy, mildly tart; used for baking, cooking. Season: November–May

Stayman. Dull red-striped skin; white flesh tinged with yellow; juicy and slightly tart; used for eating and all cooking. Season: November–April

Winesap. Bright, deep red skin; flesh tinged with yellow; very juicy and slightly tart. Used for eating and pies. Season: January–May

York Imperial. Red skin over yellow; yellowish flesh, usually lopsided; slightly tart, then flat at end of season; used for pies and baking. Season: October–March

Apricots

This delicate fruit belongs to the peach family, has the same kind of stone, and cannot be shipped when fully ripe. Most apricots come from California, Washington, or Utah and are available in June and July.

When buying, look for plump, orange-yellow fruit and avoid very firm, greenish fruit or mushy, dull-colored fruit. Ripen at room temperature if necessary. Apricots can be stored in the refrigerator from three to five days in a covered container or a perforated plastic bag. The skin of the ripe fruit strips off easily with a paring knife, but when apricots are not quite ripe they can be peeled more easily by being dipped into boiling water for 30 seconds.

Avocados (Alligator Pears)

Ranging in color from purple black to green, some avocados have a rough or leathery textured skin and others are smooth. Most of this fruit is grown in Florida and California and is generally available throughout the year.

When selecting avocados, look for bright, fresh-looking fruit that seems heavy for its size. Avoid wilted or bruised fruit and fruit with dark sunken spots and cracked or broken surfaces. Most avocados found in supermarkets require three to five days of ripening at room temperature. When soft-ripe, avocados may be stored in the warmest part of the refrigerator for three to five days.

Avocados are usually used for salads. Cut them in half, lengthwise to the seed, then twist the halves slightly, pull apart, and peel. Peeling is done most easily by making lengthwise cuts about an inch apart with a very sharp knife, barely through the skin, and then pulling off the peel.

Bananas

Unlike other fruits, bananas are harvested green and shipped while still green from the tropical countries where they grow. This means that you will find them in the supermarket throughout the year in varying degrees of ripeness, and your choice will depend upon when you wish to use them. If you wish to eat them immediately, you cannot afford to buy green bananas. Stores often offer bargains on extraripe bananas in order to sell them quickly, and if you can use these, they're a good buy. Many mothers of small children prefer to buy the small bananas, which are the right size for a child's appetite.

You can ignore two traditional bits of advice. The idea that bananas shouldn't be eaten until they have brown spots just isn't true. Many people prefer to eat bananas when they are relatively firm and still have green on the tips.

The other false idea is that bananas should *never* go into the refrigerator. It is true that bananas should be allowed to ripen at room temperature to the point at which you like to eat them. After that, they'll keep better in the refrigerator—at least a couple of days longer than in your fruit basket.

Blackberries

Blackberries must be blue black in color to be ripe; if they are red, they are "green." They, too, are served fresh with sugar and cream or with cereal; they're also used for jam, jelly, and juice. June is the season for blackberries, but they may be available from May through August. Although they grow wild all over America, New Jersey and California are the main commercial sources.

Store without washing in the refrigerator in a moisture-proof container and use within a day or two. Just before using, put them in a sieve and run cold water over them very gently—don't allow them to soak.

Blueberries

Available in June through August, most blueberries found in supermarkets are the large, cultivated varieties. They are delightful eaten fresh with sugar and cream or with cereal and may also be used in baking.

Select plump, dry, dark blueberries with a silvery bloom. They should be free of stems and leaves and uniform in size. Store blueberries in the refrigerator, covered to prevent drying out, and use in two or three days.

Cherries

Sweet cherries are slightly heart shaped, bright to deep red, white, or golden, and may be eaten raw as well as cooked. Sour or tart cherries are red to nearly black in color and are usually used for cooking. Buy cherries with a fresh ripe color. Sweet cherries should be firm; sour cherries, medium firm. Any fruits that are small, hard, or have poor color are probably less juicy and not quite ripe, whereas those that are soft, dull in color, or leaky are too ripe. Cuts or marks indicate decay.

Sweet cherries are the larger in size of the two types and are grown mostly west of the Rockies and in some parts of New York and the Great Lakes region. Depending upon the growing area, peak crops appear in the markets from May through August. Sour cherries have their peak season from June to August and are grown in the Atlantic states, with New York, Michigan, and Wisconsin as the chief producers.

Following are some of the kinds of cherries that are generally available.

SWEET CHERRIES

Bing. Extra large, heart shaped, and firm, with a dark mahogany meat and a smooth skin.

Chapman (*or Early Chapman*). Very large, round, and firm with very dark meat.

Lambert. Vary from large to extra large, are roundish with firm, very dark meat.

Republican (*or Black Republican or Lewelling*). Small to medium in size, heart shaped, and mild with dark purple meat.

Royal Ann (*or Napoleon*). Large, heart shaped, light golden, and juicy, with firm meat and skin that's easily bruised; used chiefly for canning.

Tartarian (*or Black Tartarian*). Large, heart shaped, and sweet, with dark purple meat and a thin skin.

SOUR OR TART CHERRIES

Early Richmond. First on the market, medium red with tender meat and tough skin.

English Morello. Roundish, very dark red, and tart, with dark flesh.

Montmorency. Similar to the Early Richmond, very juicy, and the most popular sour cherry; used for pies, tarts, and jellies.

Cherries are used in a variety of ways—in candies, cookies, cakes, sauces, puddings, compotes, salads, sherbets, preserves, and alcoholic beverages.

Choose top quality cherries if they are to be eaten raw or used in a decorative manner. Lesser quality is quite acceptable if they are to be chopped and mixed with other foods. Sort and throw away any spoiled cherries and then store them in the refrigerator without washing. They'll keep from three days to two weeks.

Cranberries

No one wants to be without cranberries around the Thanksgiving season, and, indeed, fall and winter is the time of year they are most readily available. Chief sources for cranberries are Massachusetts, New Jersey, Wisconsin, and Washington.

Fresh berries should be shiny, plump and firm, and bright in color. Pick over the cranberries, removing those with spots or blemishes, and store unwashed but covered in the refrigerator. They keep from one to four weeks. Cranberries are easily frozen; buy extra when they're in season and freeze in the unopened bag.

Wash cranberries before using. There are many recipes for making both uncooked and cooked cranberry relishes and desserts. These berries are very sour and generally need a lot of sugar.

Grapes

Grapes should be well formed, bright in color and firmly attached to the stem. The huge vineyards in California supply most of the fresh table grapes in the country, including the following varieties:

Almeria. Medium large, dry and firm with a greenish-white thick, tough skin; normally seeded, with neutral flavor. Season: September–November

Cardinal. A cross between the Ribier and Tokay; large, with few seeds; dark red, slightly tough skin; firm pulp, slightly pungent, sweet flavor. Season: June–August

Emperor. Large, elongated, light red, with reddish-purple thin skins; neutral flavor; normally seeded. Season: November–May

Olivette Blanche. Elongated, delicate green skin; pungent, sweet flavor; a few seeds. Season: June–August

Red Malaga. Large spherical shape; pink to reddish purple with hard crisp skin; neutral flavor; normally seeded. Season: July–October

Ribier. Round, very large; black, tough skin; meaty with medium-sweet flavor; normally seeded. Season: July–February

Thompson Seedless. Elongated, medium-sized; tender, thin, greenish-white skin; firm with neutral flavor; always seedless. Season: June–November

Tokay or Flame Tokay. Large and oval; bright red, tough, thick skin; neutral flavor; normally seeded. Season: August–January

White Malaga. Large, tough; thick greenish-white to yellow skin; neutral flavor; normally seeded. Season: September–November

Some table grapes also are grown in the eastern states, particularly in New York, Michigan, and Ohio. However, they are easily crushed and not generally shipped over long distances. They include the following varieties:

Catawba. Medium size oval; purple-red slip skin; sweet, intense flavor; seeded. Season: September–November

Concord. Medium size, blue-black slip skin; mild flavor; seeded; also used for making juice and jelly. Season: September–October

Delaware. Small, tender, light-red skin; sweet flavor, seeded and juicy. Season: August–September

Niagara. Large, round to egg shape; amber to white slip skin; juicy and seeded; sweet flavor. Season: September–October

Grapefruit

Grown chiefly in Florida, Texas, Arizona, and California, grapefruit is available throughout the year but is most plentiful from October through May. The skin color ranges from yellow and yellow green to pink. Color does not affect the quality, nor do small spots on the skin. Fruit should be firm and heavy; softened or wrinkled fruit should be avoided.

Four kinds of grapefruit are found in the market:

Burgundy. Large, with red-flushed skin; some seeds; deep pink flesh; sweet flavor. Season: November–May

Duncan. Large with smooth, pale yellow thin skin, sometimes tinged with green or russet; seeds; yellow-white flesh; fine flavor. Season: October–June

Marsh. Medium size with thin, pale yellow skin; seedless with yellowish-white flesh; tart flavor. Season: October–June

Thompson Pink (*Marsh Pink*). Small to medium; smooth, light yellow skin; seedless with pink flesh; juicy; tart flavor. Season: January–May

Grapefruits are ready to eat since only "tree ripe" fruit is allowed to be shipped. They may be kept a day or two at room temperature or should be refrigerated to avoid drying and wrinkling. A whole grapefruit can keep from one to four weeks in the refrigerator.

The most usual way to serve grapefruit is to cut it in half, remove the seeds, cut around a section to loosen it, and sweeten with sugar, honey, or jelly. Some people think that salt, rather than sugar, enhances the flavor. Serve cold with a pointed spoon or put under the broiler until slightly browned.

Lemons and Limes

Lemons may have either thick or thin all-yellow skin with pale yellow flesh. The lime has a thin green skin and light green flesh, and is slightly more acid than the lemon. Lemons are available in quantity all year. Limes also are available all year, with peak in quantity from June through August. Both fruits should be firm and fresh looking and feel heavy for their size. These fruits need not be refrigerated for the few days or weeks they are usually kept.

Both these citrus fruits are used for drinks, desserts, pies, and cakes, to season vegetables, and to sprinkle over fruit. The rind of the lemon is often grated and added to impart a special flavor to pastries, cookies, and other dishes.

Melons

This fine family of fruits includes cantaloupe, the casabas, crenshaw, honeyball and honeydew, Persian melons and watermelon. It's not always easy to buy a melon out of season, even if you are willing to pay the price.

Ripe melons can be kept in the refrigerator about a week. Unripe melons should be kept at room temperature until they are ripe and then stored in a cool place. Most people prefer to chill melon in the refrigerator several hours before serving.

With the exception of watermelon, all melons can be cut into halves, removing the seeds, and then cut into wedges and served with slices of lime or lemon. A half cantaloupe often is served with other fruits or ice cream in the center.

All of the melons can be cut into 1-inch cubes, with rind removed, and used in salads or with other fruits. Melon flesh can also be pickled or made into preserves.

Following are some specifics about each of these melons:

Cantaloupes (*Muskmelons*). Small and oval shaped, they have a rind that is coarse and rather heavily ridged (with ridges netting crosswise) and are grayish with a light background. When you cut these melons open, the inside edible part is salmon colored with a rather pungent aroma and a sweet taste when fully ripe.

Because cantaloupes are picked for shipping before full maturity, they are still quite firm when freshly displayed in stores. For their best eating stage, hold them several days at room temperature until they take on a yellow appearance and acquire a distinctive aroma. Cantaloupes are generally available from May through September. Wrap for storage to keep their pungent odor from penetrating the refrigerator.

Casabas. Quite large, and shaped rather like a globe, they sometimes have a slight point at the blossom end. The rind is rather rough, furrowed but with no criss-cross netting, and yellow in color. The edible flesh is creamy white with very little color, and has a taste that is sweet and juicy. The riper the melon, the deeper the yellow color. This melon is available from July to November, with peak quantities in September and October.

Crenshaws. As large as casabas, they have a more pointed stem end. The rind is quite smooth and a green-gold color. The flesh inside, however, is salmon colored and is juicy with a spicy taste. When quite ripe, the blossom end is very soft and the rind dark. The Crenshaws are on the market from July to October.

Honeydews. Quite large (4 to 8 pounds) and sometimes shaped like footballs, they have a rind that is usually velvety smooth but may sometimes be slightly netted. Ripe honeydews are creamy white to creamy yellow on the outside, the flesh inside is a light green with a very faint fragrance. They are flavorfully sweet and juicy, making them especially desirable for desserts. Dead-white melons, especially with a greenish tinge, are immature and will not sweeten. Honeydews have the best flavor when served at room temperature. A similar melon, the *honeyball,* has many of the same characteristics as the honeydew except that it is much smaller, is very round, and is irregularly netted over the surface. Both are available from June to October.

Persians. Shaped rather like a cantaloupe but a bit larger, their rind has a very even, fine netting over a deep green background. The flesh is orange-pink, with a pleasing aroma and a mildly sweet taste. The rind color lightens and the blossom end becomes soft when ripe. They are available from July to October.

Watermelons. The largest of all melons, they are symmetrical and oblong or round in shape. The most common is the oblong type, weighing from 25 to 40 pounds, with a smooth skin that is deep green to greenish gray and yellowish on the underside where the fruit rests on the ground. The flesh is pink or red, extremely juicy and sweet and the seeds are dark brown or black. There are many other varieties, yellow and white, as well as red, with seeds that can be brown, black, green, red, or white. In all types, though, the flesh is quite sweet and has a very high water content.

Watermelons have been grown in this country for hundreds of years, starting, strangely enough, in the northern state of Massachusetts. However, they are most successfully raised in warm southern climates and are available from May through September, though peak supplies come in June, July, and August. You will find them sold halved, quartered, or by the slice, as well as whole, in most markets. A good watermelon will be symmetrical in shape, firm, and solid. It matters little whether it's long like a football or round like a cannonball; the taste is the same.

An uncut watermelon will keep well over a week in the refrigerator, but if it's cut, the surface should be covered with moisture-proof paper and only stored for a day or two.

Watermelons are best if chilled before serving and can be eaten either in slices with the skin attached or cut into small pieces, with the skin removed, and added to other melons and fruits. Fresh lime or lemon juice takes away some of the sweetness.

Oranges

Half of the world's supply of oranges is produced in California, Florida, Texas, and Arizona. A good share of these oranges are destined to serve as the typical American breakfast juice. Fresh oranges are available the year round, with peak supplies from December to May.

There are many varieties of oranges. They include:

Valencia. A leading variety from California and Arizona, it has rich orange skin color and is excellent either for juicing or slicing in salads. It is available from late April through October. Valencias are also grown in Florida and Texas. Marketed from late March through June.

Navel. Also from California and Arizona, it has a thicker somewhat more pebbled skin than the Valencia. The skin is more easily removed by hand, and the segments separate more readily. It is ideally suited for eating as a whole fruit or as segments in salads and desserts. On the market from November until early May.

Hamlin and Parson Brown. These are early varieties of the thin-skinned sweet oranges grown in Florida and Texas that chiefly are used for juice. Available from early October until late June.

Pineapple Orange. Another high quality orange from Florida and Texas, it is good for hand eating. Available from late November through March.

Temple. A Florida-grown orange that is somewhat like the California navel orange in that it peels easily, separates into segments readily, and has excellent flavor. On the market from early December until early March.

Skin color is not an indication of quality. All oranges, as required by law, must be well matured before being harvested and shipped out of the producing state. Thus, a greenish or brownish color does not mean an orange is immature or of poor quality. Some oranges are artificially colored, but such fruit is stamped "color added" and the coloring is harmless. In general, oranges should be firm and heavy for their size, without soft or discolored spots, cuts, or skin punctures. Oranges may be kept at room temperature or kept cold and used as desired.

Peaches

This fruit is next in popularity to the apple and orange. Peaches have a fuzzy velvety skin and are fairly round in shape. There are many varieties—with yellow flesh or white flesh; freestone (flesh readily separates from the pit) or clingstone (flesh clings tightly to the pit). Freestones are usually preferred for eating fresh and for freezing; clingstones are used primarily for commercial canning, although they sometimes appear on local markets.

Peaches are harvested from May to October along the Pacific coast, on the Atlantic coast from Georgia to New Hampshire, and in New York, Ohio, and Michigan. Peaches should be plump-looking, fairly firm or becoming a trifle soft, and creamy or yellowish in color, with red blush. This fruit will not ripen well if it's been picked green and immature, but instead will shrivel or become flabby. Overripe fruit bruises easily and should be used immediately.

Peaches should be refrigerated unwashed and will keep for up to two weeks. If the fruit is hard to peel, 30 seconds in boiling water will make the skin come off quite easily. Cut peaches should be sprinkled with lemon juice to keep them from turning brown.

Pears

In contrast to peaches, pears are improved by being picked while still hard and allowed to ripen at room temperature. Buy pears that are fairly firm, plump-looking, and free from bruises, and eat them while still firm. Pears ripen from the inside out and should not be held until soft on the outside, for at that stage they are becoming somewhat mushy and tasteless. When ripe, keep cold and humid and eat as soon as possible.

The main varieties, all grown in Washington, Oregon and California, are:

Anjou. Quite large, with a green or greenish yellow skin when ripe, sometimes blending into deep rose. An all-purpose pear, it has a winey flavor and is available from October to May.

Bartlett. The most popular variety and produced in great quantities for both fresh fruit and for commercial canning. It is an all-purpose pear of medium size and is yellow with a red blush when ripe. They develop a delightful fragrance when ready to eat. Bartlett pears are available from early August through November.

Bosc. Has a slightly acid taste, a very large tapering neck, and is dark greenish yellow to brownish yellow, overlaid with a cinnamon-color russeting, characteristic of this type of pear. Although good for eating, it's especially good for cooking and baking, and is available November to May.

Comice. Definitely an eating pear. It is large, roundish with greenish-yellow to yellow-red skin, and is available October to January.

Seckel. Quite small, yellowish-brown and spicy in flavor. It's used for pickling as well as eating and canning, and is available from September to December.

Pineapple

Most of the pineapple sold in our fresh fruit markets is imported from Puerto Rico and Mexico, although a small amount comes from Hawaii. It's available all year, with the peak season from March through June.

Buy fruit that is heavy for its size and as large as possible. The larger the fruit, the greater the proportion of edible flesh. Avoid green fruit or that which is overripe. Check the bottom for any indications of decay. Crown leaves should be fresh and deep green. Don't buy fruit with brown leaves or indications of dryness. Also avoid fruit with soft spots or sunken pips (eyes).

When fully ripe, pineapples are golden yellow, orange-yellow, or reddish brown, depending upon the variety. Use as soon as possible, although pineapples will keep in the refrigerator for two to three days.

The usual way to prepare pineapple is to remove the leaves, cut the fruit into 1-inch-thick rings, and core and pare. The rings can be served whole or cut into smaller pieces. This fruit should be sweet enough to eat without sugar.

Plums

These fruits vary in shape from round to oval and in skin colors—blue, green, yellow, purple, or red. They also vary in taste from sweet to tart.

Italian (*Prune Plum*). Blue purple with sweet firm flesh and good to eat raw. Also used for home canning and preserves.

Damson. Quite small and usually purple. There is a yellow Damson plum called the mirabelle and there is also the greengage plum which is small, round, greenish yellow, with a sharp sweet taste.

Japanese. Yellow with red overtones, heart shaped, firm and sweet.

Fresh plums can be bought from June through September, with some of the imported ones (from South America) available from January through March.

Because there are so many varieties, color is not an indication of quality, but the plums should be smooth and in fairly firm to slightly soft stage of ripeness, with no cracks or wrinkled skin. Too soft fruit tends to be too ripe. Unripe plums can be ripened at room temperature and then stored in the refrigerator, covered, but use them as soon as possible.

Raspberries

These fruits grow on wild and cultivated bushes all over the United States and are available from June to November, but the peak month is July. We think of them as being red in color, but they may be purple, black, or amber. The berry itself is made up of many tiny, delicately flavored droplets. They may be eaten raw or with cream and sugar, or be used in jellies and jams or in place of strawberries in almost any recipe.

Berries should be solid, plump, and fresh. If the berries are leaking juice, it means they are overripe and/or damaged. Berries should be sorted, bad ones discarded, and refrigerated, unwashed, to be used within one or two days.

The berries should be rinsed quickly in cold water just before using. Do not allow them to soak, and gently shake them dry.

Rhubarb

This plant has a thick red and green stalk over a foot long, with a large green leaf on top. Only the stalk is used in cooking (never eat the leaves). Easily grown in all parts of the United States, rhubarb is the first fresh fruit available in the spring and is on the market from January through June.

It's sold either by the bunch or by weight. The stalks should be firm and crisp with a bright red color. Rhubarb is quite perishable and should be refrigerated immediately and used in one to three days.

The simplest and most usual way to prepare rhubarb is to cut off the leaves and stem ends. The stalk is cut into inch-long pieces and put in a saucepan with enough water to barely cover, and cooked until tender. Sugar is added to taste, but quite a lot is generally required as rhubarb is a very tart fruit. It may be eaten either warm or cold. Rhubarb pie is a perennial favorite.

Strawberries

Look for berries of medium size, of uniform color and shape, and with caps and stems still in place. Very large berries are likely to lack flavor, and small, misshapen berries tend to be bitter. The best berries will have a solid red color and very little white or green on them. Stained containers are likely to indicate leakage and spoilage.

As strawberries are highly perishable, plan to use them immediately. Don't try to store them longer than a day or two without freezing them. They are available all year, but April through June is the peak supply period and prices are likely to be best then.

Tangelos

Actually a hybrid of mandarin oranges and grapefruit, tangelos have an excellent taste all of their own. The best fruit is firm, heavy for its size, thin-skinned, and light orange in color. Tangelos may be kept at room temperature or stored in the refrigerator. They are on the market from late October through January.

Tangerines

About the best indicator of ripe, flavorable fruit is a deep orange or almost red color and a bright luster. Tangerines should feel heavy for their size, but a puffy appearance is typical as the skin practically zips off, and the segments are easily separated. Tangerines are very perishable and should be kept cold and used as soon as possible. Florida is the chief source of tangerines. They are on the market chiefly from November through January.

Vegetables

In general, one of the best ways of preserving the maximum food values in fresh vegetables is to cook them until tender with only enough water to prevent scorching. For most vegetables it's important to use a tight-fitting lid to keep the steam from escaping and to help the vegetables cook more quickly. Green vegetables should be cooked uncovered, however, for three minutes to let gases which cause them to darken escape. After the three-minute cooking period, cover and finish cooking to the desired degree of tenderness.

Artichokes

The size of the artichoke has nothing to do with its quality, but the larger it is the more you get for your money because you usually buy by the unit rather than by the pound. The leaves should be compact, tightly closed, plump, and green. Loose-spreading or discolored leaves are a sign of poor quality and overmaturity.

Artichokes should be used as soon as possible but may be stored in the refrigerator in a covered container or plastic bag for four days.

To prepare, cut off the stem and one inch across the top. Clip off the thorny tips with a scissors. Drop into a bowl of water with a few tablespoons of lemon juice or vinegar to keep edges from turning brown until ready to cook. Pull off any loose leaves around the bottom.

To cook; place in boiling, salted water and cook uncovered until tender. This varies from 15 to 45 minutes depending on the size of the artichoke. Test by pressing the stem with a fork. One artichoke serves one person and can be eaten either hot or cold with a variety of sauces.

Asparagus

Tender asparagus has straight green brittle stalks that break easily. Tips that have begun to spread show overmaturity; stalks that are wilted, thin, or crooked may be tough or stringy. The peak market season for asparagus starts in mid-February (California) and continues through June (New Jersey).

Do not wash until just before cooking. Unwashed stalks can be stored in the refrigerator in a covered container for four days.

To prepare: wash thoroughly in cold running water to remove all sand. Break off the tough lower portion of stem.

To cook: whole asparagus is boiled for 10 to 20 minutes, whereas the tips alone will take only 5 or 10 minutes. Remember to cook uncovered for first three minutes. Asparagus can be eaten hot or cold with a variety of sauces and can be used in salads, casseroles, and cream soups.

Beans (Snap)

The green, podded varieties are generally available throughout the year, but yellow wax beans and large green pole beans also are found occasionally. In choosing fresh beans, pick slender ones. Large bumps mean large seeds which can be tough and mealy. The length is not important. Look for crisp beans that are free from scars and avoid any with dry-looking pods. Snap beans may be stored washed or unwashed for three to five days in a covered container in the refrigerator.

To prepare: snap off the ends. If the bean has a "string" it will come off with the stem end. Use whole, snap, or cut into inch-size pieces. There is a special bean slicer for making French style beans.

To cook: place beans in about an inch of boiling salted water. Bring the water to a boil again, cook for three minutes, then cover, and cook over medium heat for ten to fifteen minutes. After

10 minutes sample the beans to see if they have reached the tender, crisp stage.

Beans may be served hot by themselves, creamed, or combined with other vegetables, or in soups, stews, and casseroles. Cold beans are good in salads. One pound of beans will make five one-half cup servings.

Beets

Choose only deep, red colored beets of uniform size, with no ridges or blemishes. Don't buy any with soft spots. If the beets are sold with the tops, the tops should be fresh and green. If these are still tender, they can be cooked the way spinach is cooked.

Beets can be stored covered in the refrigerator for one to two weeks.

To prepare: cut off the green tops and scrub the beets with a soft brush.

To cook: young, small whole beets are boiled from 30 to 45 minutes; larger, older whole beets, 45 to 90 minutes; sliced or diced beets, 15 to 25 minutes. Put the beets in one inch of boiling salted water and heat again to boiling point. Cover and cook until tender, drain, and run cold water over them to facilitate pulling off the skins.

One and one-half pounds of beets (without tops) make about six servings.

Broccoli

This is a dark green relative of the cauliflower, but most of the stem can be eaten as well as the flowerets. Buy only heads that are quite dark green or have a slightly purplish cast. Heads that are starting to "flower" or turn yellowish are too mature.

Fresh broccoli can be stored in the refrigerator, covered, up to three or four days.

To prepare: cut off the larger leaves and the tough bottom of the main stem. Make lengthwise cuts through the bottoms of the remaining stems so they'll cook as quickly as the flowerets. Rinse thoroughly.

To cook: broccoli can be steamed by tying a bunch together loosely and standing them upright in a pot of 1 inch of boiling salted water for 10 to 15 minutes. It can be cooked as a crisp "Chinesy" vegetable if cut in small pieces and sautéed in hot fat. Cut-up broccoli can be cooked in one inch boiling salted water. Put stem pieces in first and bring to a boil. Cook for 3 minutes, then cover and cook for 7 to 12 minutes. Drain before serving.

Serve broccoli hot with butter, lemon, or other sauces; use cold in salads and for casseroles. Two pounds of broccoli provides six servings.

Brussels Sprouts

These members of the cabbage family look like tiny cabbages, about the size of a large walnut or a ping pong ball. They're available about ten months of the year, but the peak market is from October through December. They are usually sold as a unit in pint-sized boxes that can be stored in the refrigerator for up to four days. The smaller they are, the better they taste. The sprouts should be firm and green, with no yellow or discolored leaves.

To prepare: just before using wash well in cold water, trim off a bit of the stem and any loose or discolored leaves.

To cook: boil in a very small amount of salted water for three minutes uncovered, then cover and cook for three to eight minutes until tender. Overcooking can cause them to have a strong, unpleasant flavor. Drain and season with butter. One pound yields four servings.

Cabbage

There are many different kinds of cabbage on the market all year in large amounts. In general, the leaves should be solid and well packed and the heads should seem heavy for their size. Don't buy heads that have wilted or discolored outer leaves. Raw, uncut cabbage can be covered and kept in the refrigerator for seven to eight days. Different varieties of cabbage are available all year. They include:

Danish. Very solid, late maturing, with the leaves tight and

smooth across the top, and with heads that are round but somewhat flattened.

Domestic. Heads are a little less compact than the Danish, the
leaves slightly curled and not overlapping as far across the top.

Green or New. Smaller head than either Danish or domestic
and a deeper green color.

Red cabbage. Similar to green except it is reddish-purple in
color. It is especially attractive in tossed salads.

Savoy. Very crinkled leaves, shading from dark to pale green,
and a loosely formed head. It has a milder flavor than other cabbages and is in demand for slaws and salads.

Cabbage can be cooked or eaten raw. It should never be overcooked. Finely shredded raw cabbage is used for cole slaw and may
be added to tossed salads.

To cook: cabbage cut into wedges should be cooked in an inch
of boiling salted water in a large pot. Add the wedges, boil uncovered for two to three minutes, cover pan and simmer for ten
to twelve minutes more. It should be tender but still crisp. Cabbage
can be shredded and boiled the same way but should cook for
only five to eight minutes. Drain and season with melted butter
if you wish. Grated nutmeg is also good on cabbage.

Carrots

There's never a time of year you can't buy carrots. Major
crops are grown from California to Florida, and depending on
climate and variety, you'll find carrots that are long, thin, and
tapered, or that are short, thick, and stubby, or shapes between
the two. The only thing to remember is that a limp carrot is a
very old carrot; fresh ones are nice and firm. A carrot that is too
large is likely to have a sharp, unpleasant taste. Very tiny new
carrots are tender and sweet, but the smaller they are the more
time is involved in cleaning them.

Buy only nicely shaped, bright orange carrots, avoiding those
with bumps or cracks. It is not possible, of course, to examine
carrots if packaged in 1- or 2-pound plastic bags, but these have
the advantage of being washed, tops removed, and ready to store

in your refrigerator. Carrots are rarely found now with their green tops left on because this additional bulk increases shipping costs. Carrots, like all other vegetables, should be used as soon as possible but will keep fresh in your refrigerator for several weeks.

Carrots are as frequently eaten raw, cut in strips, or shredded in salads as they are cooked.

To prepare: scrub small carrots with a vegetable brush, cutting off the top and a bit of the tip. Larger ones are more easily cleaned with a carrot scraper (also called a potato peeler).

To cook: carrots can be cooked whole or cut either into strips lengthwise or into round slices. (Lengthwise cutting preserves more nutrients.) Add carrots to one inch of boiling salted water in a sauce pan, cover, and cook until tender; drain and serve with butter or other seasonings. Whole carrots cook in 20 to 30 minutes; quartered or sliced in 15 to 20 minutes; diced or sliced in 10 to 15 minutes.

Cauliflower

This vegetable transports and keeps quite well. It is grown in many states, with the largest crops coming from New York and California. The peak supply is from September through January.

Buy cauliflower with a firm, tight head, and clean, white flowerets. The quality of cauliflower is the same for a large head as it is for a small head, and if leaves have grown through the flowerets, or curd, as this is sometimes called, it does not affect the taste. But don't buy a head with curd that looks a bit grainy, or rice-like, or with leaves that are yellowed or withered. Fresh, raw cauliflower will keep in your refrigerator for four to five days.

To prepare: cut off the heavy outer leaves and the woody base. Sometimes on very large heads there is discoloration in the center of the base. This core should be cut out.

To cook: put cauliflower in about an inch of boiling, salted water for about five minutes, uncovered, then cover. A whole head cooks in about 15 or 20 minutes, and flowerets, in 5 to 10 minutes. A little lemon juice in the water helps keep the cauliflower white, but if it is overcooked it will still discolor.

You don't have to cook a whole head of cauliflower at once; store what you want for another day in a plastic bag. Leftover cooked cauliflower can be covered and kept in the refrigerator for one to four days and used in such dishes as cauliflower soufflé or baked in a casserole with a cheese sauce.

Raw cauliflower makes good bite-sized pieces to eat with a "dip," and in smaller pieces is a good crunchy addition to green salads.

Celery

There are several different varieties of celery in the supermarket, but by far the most common is the Pascal type. Look for outer stalks with a standard clipped length and fresh green leaves. Avoid bunches that have cracked, bruised, or loosened stalks.

Another variety is the *Golden Heart,* a blanched white celery grown under paper to prevent chlorophyll from forming and turning it green. Usually more expensive, its nutritional value is about the same as the Pascal type.

Celeriac, sometimes referred to as celery root or celery knob, is a variety of celery. It has dark, turnip-like roots, which should be clean and free from damage. Only the root is eaten. Americans seldom eat it raw.

Celery hearts, which many stores carry, are simply the tender, inner branches of the Pascal or Golden varieties of celery.

Remember that the celery leaves and the somewhat tougher outer stalks of the celery are very nutritious and are good to use in soups and stews. It's helpful to clean the celery as soon as you bring it home from the store and then separate it for cooking or eating-out-of-hand or salad purposes.

Available year round, celery lends itself to varied cooking methods, including boiling, braising, and frying as well as the conventional ways of serving it raw.

Corn

August is the peak season for sweet corn in most states, but fresh corn is available from May through December. Buy corn in the husks if possible. These should be bright green, tight to the cob, with dark-brown silk at the end. The kernels should be in even rows, with no space between, and firm enough to resist a slight pressure. Most fresh corn on the market is yellow and has higher vitamin A content than the white variety.

As texture, flavor, and much sugar content is lost within 24 hours after picking, corn should be used as soon as possible. It can be stored in the refrigerator, but the husks should not be removed until just before cooking.

To prepare and cook: a dry vegetable brush comes in handy for removing any silk that may stick to the corn. Rinse in cold water and plunge the ears into a large kettle with enough boiling water to cover the ears. This water should not be salted. Cover and boil rapidly for 5 to 10 minutes—less for freshly picked corn. Drain and serve with butter, salt, and pepper.

Cucumbers

Available all year, the peak crop of cucumbers is from May to August. There is no state that does not grow this popular member of the gourd family. Buy cucumbers that are nicely shaped, firm, and bright green in color. Cucumbers turning yellow and puffy are overripe, and those with a shriveled skin are tough and bitter.

Cucumbers may be washed and dried and stored in the refrigerator for from one to two weeks. If you wish to peel them, wait until you are ready to use them. Cucumbers are usually used raw for appetizers and in salads or sandwiches. Very thinly sliced cucumbers that have been marinated for several hours in a mixture of vinegar, sugar, salt, and pepper are a spicy, fresh accompaniment to a dinner.

Eggplant

Available the year round, eggplants come in small, medium, and large sizes. Your choice will depend upon your recipe plan and the number of servings you need. Eggplants of any size should be firm and smooth, with a shiny, dark purple color, slightly oblong or egg shaped, and from 6 to 9 inches in diameter. Any brown, rough, or spongy spot on the skin will very quickly spoil the whole eggplant.

Eggplants can be stored in the refrigerator, from three days to two weeks; otherwise they should be used as quickly as possible.

To prepare and cook: wash thoroughly, but don't soak. Take the skin off if you like, but if it's tender, it has an exceptionally nice flavor. One way of preparing eggplant is to deep-fry it. Peel the eggplant and cut it into sticks about ½ inch thick. Sprinkle with salt and pepper, toss in flour, and dip into a dish containing an egg beaten up with a little milk. Roll in bread crumbs and fry in hot fat until golden brown. Spread out on an absorbent paper and serve while hot.

Endive, Chicory, and Escarole

Used primarily in salads, these vegetables are available most of the year. Endive or chicory—which name you use depends upon where you live—has long, very curly-edged tendrils branching from main stems. These are very dark green at the edges, shading to pale green in the center. Escarole has much broader, dark green leaves that are less crinkly than those of curly endive or chicory. In buying, look for freshness, crispness, and good green color of the outer leaves. Because of their curly leaves, these greens need thorough washing. Their somewhat bitter tang combines nicely with milder greens in a tossed salad.

Belgian, or *Witloof,* endive is a small, compact, cigar-shaped plant which is creamy white from being grown in complete darkness. Very delicate and perishable, and therefore expensive, it may be used raw in salads or braised for a vegetable side dish.

Greens

The many different plants known as greens include *kale, collards, turnip tops, Swiss chard, beet greens, mustard greens,* and *spinach* (see separate listing).

Look for greens which appear fresh, young, and tender and have a good, healthy green color. Avoid any dry or yellowing leaves, greens which seem wilted, or those which show any sign of insect damage. Keep cool and moist and use as soon as possible.

To prepare: wash carefully in running water and discard any damaged leaves. However, try to use as many of the outer leaves as possible because they have higher nutritive value. The stems and woody midribs of leaves may be removed before cooking to decrease the cooking time.

To cook: place in a small amount of boiling salted water, cook uncovered for three minutes, reduce heat (just keep water boiling), and cook covered until just tender and slightly crisp. For greater color and milder flavor, cook uncovered with enough water to cover the vegetable after it has wilted during the first few minutes of cooking.

Lettuce

This basic salad ingredient comes in many varieties—some lettuce even has reddish leaves—and is available in one variety or another all year. Four types of lettuce are generally sold.

Iceberg. The major type, sometimes called crisp head, it is available all year in large amounts. It has large, round, solid heads, with medium-green outer leaves and lighter green or pale-green inner leaves that are quite tightly folded together. This lettuce is often used in sandwiches as well as in salads.

Butterhead. This term includes the *Bibb* and *Boston* lettuce varieties; smaller, looser heads than iceberg lettuce, shaping into a rosette pattern in the center. The leaves are light green, quite smooth, soft and tender rather than crisp. Bibb lettuce heads are smaller and more cup-shaped than those of the Boston variety.

Romaine or Cos. Tall, cylindrically shaped and long, its dark-green leaves are crisper than most other lettuce varieties and shaped into a loosely folded head.

Leaf lettuce. This type does not form a compact head. Often called *garden* lettuce, there are many varieties grown mainly in greenhouses or on truck farms and sold locally. The leaves are broad, tender, and curled to smooth and vary in color from pale green to dark green to reddish color, depending upon the variety.

When buying iceberg and romaine, look particularly for clean, crisp leaves, with no ragged brown areas. Heads of iceberg should be fairly firm. Butterhead and loose-leaf lettuce should be clean, fresh, and tender, with no wilting.

All lettuce should be refrigerated as soon as possible. If you have the time, it's best to wash it thoroughly, drain it well, and put it in a large plastic bag to store in the refrigerator. Most fresh greens will keep from three to four days to a week.

For head lettuce, turn it upside down, twist out the core or cut it out with a knife. Hold it under cold, running water, which will not only clean but spread the leaves apart. Drain it upside down in a colander or put it in a dry, clean kitchen towel and shake out the water before putting it in the refrigerator to crisp or store.

Greens used in a salad should be quite dry so that the salad dressing will adhere to the leaves. Blot them with paper towels if necessary. Tear greens in pieces rather than cutting them, for cutting will cause the edges to darken. Add the dressing to the salad just before you are ready to serve, and, of course, don't use too much or you'll have a limp salad.

Mushrooms

Many thousands of varieties of mushrooms grow in the United States, in shapes, colors, and sizes that defy the imagination. The only thing all mushrooms have in common is that they are a fungus and get their nourishment from living or dead plants. They cannot manufacture chlorophyll, so you'll never see a green one.

Of all the edible mushrooms, the only species cultivated commercially in this country is the *Agaricus campestris*. Bought fresh, they should be white to creamy white with firm tops and pale beige stems. The fluted section under the top, called gills, should be light in color. Brown or black gills indicate old age. These mushrooms have tops, or caps as they're called, between ¾ of an inch and 3 inches in diameter.

Fresh mushrooms should be stored unwashed in a shallow pan and covered with a damp towel; air should be able to circulate around them. Stored this way in the refrigerator, they will keep about a week.

To prepare: just before using, wash mushrooms quickly in cold water and pat dry—don't ever soak. Mushrooms do not need to be peeled and can be either sautéed whole or cut in pieces. If you wish, the stems can be used for soups or gravies, the caps, as a special vegetable or, if large enough, garnished with a topping of some sort and baked.

Mushrooms turn dark if cut and not prepared promptly. A little lemon juice prevents them from darkening during cooking.

Okra

This controversial vegetable is the immature seed pod of the okra plant. People are either crazy about it or go out of their way to avoid it. In the southern states, where it's grown and marketed locally all year, it's sometimes called *gumbo* because it's used to flavor and thicken gumbos and soups. In the northern states okra is on the market from May to October.

Some okra pods are long and thin, others are short and thick, and the color can vary from whitish-green to green. Pods may be smooth or ridged but should always be purchased when young, tender, crisp, and not over 4 inches in length. They should snap easily and be without hard seeds.

Okra can be washed, shaken dry, and stored in a covered container in the refrigerator for three to five days.

To cook: small pods can be cooked whole; large pods should have their stems cut off and be cut into 1-i .: slices. Okra can be boiled for 10 to 15 minutes in a very small amount of boiling salted water and then drained and served seasoned with butter, salt, and pepper. Overcooked okra tends to be gummy.

Onions

There are many different kinds of onions—different in size, shape, color, and flavor—but all belong to the lily, or bulb, family. They are marketed both fresh and dry and are in good supply in many forms the year round.

The fresh or green onions and related vegetables include:

Green onions. Also known as spring onions, they are ordinary onions harvested very young when their bulbs have reached a diameter of from one-fourth of an inch to one inch. *Scallions* are very young green onions that have no bulb formation. Both are on the market all year, with greatest supply from May to August, and are much desired for appetizers and for salads.

Leeks. These look like overgrown green onions with large, flat, dark-green leaves. The leaves are juicy and the entire leek has a pleasing mild onion flavor. Sold in bunches, they are cooked and served in much the same way as asparagus. Peak availability is September through November and in the spring.

Shallots. These are also like green onions but grow in rosy, pink clusters, similar to garlic cloves. Shallots of good quality have fresh green tops; they are available in fresh form in November through April.

Chives. Thin, grasslike blades with delicate flavor. They are sold in clumps or little pots and snipped off with a scissors to be used as needed for flavoring and garnishing.

In buying fresh onions, look for fresh, clean bunches with green tops; avoid yellowed, wilted or badly damaged tops, which are a sign of age. Wash carefully and peel away any bruised leaves. Keep cold and humid in the refrigerator and use as soon as possible.

The dry or mature types of onions have a dry, paper-thin outer skin by the time they reach the market. In general, they are best when they are clean, hard, and well shaped, and it is advisable to buy in quantities that meet your immediate needs. Store in a cool, dry place.

Dry onions can be classified into mild-sweet and dry-strong types.

Bermudas. Thick and flat in shape, with red, white, or tan skin; they are sweet, mild, and juicy. Available from March through June, they are good sliced raw into salads or sandwiches or fried in deep fat.

Spanish. Larger than Bermudas, sometimes 3 inches in diameter, these onions have globe-like shapes and white, light yellow, or tan skin. Also sweet, mild, and juicy, they are in peak supply from August through April.

White. Sometimes called boiling onions, these silvery-skinned onions are small (1 to 1½ inches across) and globe shaped and are served creamed or with butter as a vegetable or used for stews and meat pies.

Yellow. Dry and strong, this onion is in good supply the year round in small, medium, and large sizes for use as an ingredient or flavoring agent in many types of recipes.

Red or Italian. Medium sized and oval-shaped, these pungent onions add flavor and color sliced into salads and sandwiches.

Parsnips

This old-fashioned root vegetable is primarily a late winter vegetable. It is mostly on the market October through April because its flavor is sweeter and more desirable after prolonged exposure to cold temperatures (40° F. or below). They should be smooth, firm, and well formed, and those of small or medium size are more desirable than larger parsnips, which may have woody or pithy cores.

To cook: use the methods for storing and cooking carrots for parsnips. Scrape, slice into lengthwise strips, and boil or steam in a covered pan for 15 to 20 minutes if boiled and 30 to 40 minutes if steamed.

Peas

Fresh green peas are not commonly found in the market any more, except locally in season. They must be young and kept cool from harvesting to table, as they lose sweetness and tenderness quickly. Pods should be uniformly green, shiny clean, and snap open easily.

To cook: as soon after shelling as possible, cook, uncovered to preserve greenness, in as little water as possible and for as short a time as possible, not more than 8 to 10 minutes. Peas may be cooked in combination with onions, carrots, and mushrooms, or in cream sauce. They are good in rice dishes, served alongside mashed potatoes, and made into pea soup. Small raw "sweet" peas are excellent in salads.

Peppers, Sweet

The most common variety is the green bell pepper, which is about 4 to 5 inches long and has 3 or 4 lobes. Red peppers are sometimes available and are slightly sweeter. Peppers are on the market all year but are most plentiful during the late summer.

Look for peppers that are bright green or red, have a shiny skin, and feel relatively heavy in relation to their size. Avoid any that are wilted, flabby, or have flimsy, thin walls.

To cook: simply remove the stem and seeds and slice or dice to add flavor and color to salads, casseroles, and scrambled eggs, or parboil for five minutes and stuff them with a mixture of meat, seafood, or poultry for a main dish.

Potatoes

Potatoes are in abundant supply throughout the year. Russet Burbank, or "russet," potatoes are often identified in the store by that name, although most potatoes are identified by their state of origin. Russets are long and oval and have a netted surface. They often are identified as coming from Idaho or another far western state, although sizable quantities also come from Maine. They are generally regarded as tops for baking and french fries because they have a grainy texture when cooked. They are usually higher priced than the long white (or "California") varieties, the red potatoes (Red Bliss or Pontiacs), and the most common, and usually lowest priced, round whites.

The most common round white potato varieties are Katahdin, Kennebec, Irish Cobbler, and Chippewa, but variety names are often omitted, and just the grower-shipper's address is used for identification. These are usually the best buys for general purposes.

Depending on the season of the year, "new" potatoes—those which are freshly dug and on the smallish and slightly immature side—may be available. They are excellent when creamed.

Nearly all supermarket potatoes are "U.S. No. 1" grade, which is assurance of freedom from defects. The permitted size range, however, is great, and it will take study to learn which brand packs more uniform sizes. Uniformity is important if you expect all the potatoes to finish baking at the same time.

In general, fresh potatoes should be quite firm, not wrinkled or leathery-looking, and should be free from greenish spots or sprouting. Store potatoes in a cool, dark, well-ventilated place. This is especially necessary for the new potatoes.

To prepare and cook: to retain the maximum nutrients, many vitamin-conscious cooks scrub potatoes well but leave the skins on. If potatoes are peeled, the paring should be very thin. Remove the eyes with the tip of a sharp knife.

In general, potatoes should be cooked in a covered pan in 1 inch of boiling salted water, preferably with skins on. Medium-sized potatoes take 25 to 30 minutes. Small, new potatoes, or peeled and cut-up pieces of potato will cook in a little less time. Test for doneness with a fork; potatoes shouldn't have a "bone" in the middle.

To make mashed potatoes, peel the potatoes, cut them into halves or quarters, place them in 1 inch of lightly salted water, and cook in a covered pan until easily pierced with a fork. Don't overcook or they will be mushy. Drain off the water, which can be saved for soups, and dry the potatoes slightly by shaking the pan over low heat. Mash with a hand masher or an electric mixer, adding a small amount of hot milk or cream and butter or margarine. Season to taste and beat until the potatoes are fluffy and lump-free. Leftover mashed potatoes can be fried as patties in butter or used as topping for a meat casserole.

Any potato can be baked, although the Idaho is fluffiest and easiest to scoop out and refill. Scrub the potatoes well, take out the eyes, rub all over with a little shortening, and bake in an oven preheated to 450° F. on a thin metal pan or directly on the oven rack. They should be done in 45 to 50 minutes, although new potatoes take longer. Before serving, cut a gash along one side and squeeze (holding it with a clean towel) until the potato pops through the top. Add a pat of butter or a dollop of sour cream, perhaps with chives.

Radishes

Most commonly available in the markets throughout the year are the small round red radishes, but you may also see elongated red and white ones or round white ones.

Radishes should be smooth and firm, without black spots or pitting. Very large or flabby radishes are likely to have pithy centers and poor flavor. Most are sold in bags with the tops removed, but if the tops have not been removed, they should be fresh and green-looking. They, too, may be eaten.

To prepare: simply wash them with a vegetable brush and remove tops and root ends. Slice them thinly for salads or serve
them whole with salt, the way our grandmothers did, or with
sweet butter as the French do.

Spinach

Although spinach has already been mentioned under "greens,"
it's about the most widely available of that group. Spinach is sold
either in bulk by the pound or already washed and trimmed in
plastic bags. Leaves are either flat or curly but should be large,
crisp, and dark green. Wilted or blemished leaves should be
avoided.

To prepare: even already washed spinach should be washed
again. All stems and roots should be trimmed away and the leaves
washed in a large container of slightly warm water. (If the water
is warm, the sand in the leaves is removed more easily.) Lift spinach out of the water so any silt will remain in it. Wash two or three
more times in cold, running water. Shake dry in a sieve or colander
and store in a plastic bag or other covered container in the refrigerator, where it will keep for three to five days.

To cook: the modern method for cooking spinach utilizes only
the water that adheres to the leaves. Place the cleaned leaves in
the pot, cover, and cook for five to eight minutes. Serve drained
and seasoned with salt and pepper or a little lemon juice. Leftover spinach may be used in a variety of pies, casseroles, and
egg and cheese dishes.

Squash

Squash comes in all sorts of shapes, sizes, and colors. Although
frequently classified as "summer" and "winter" squash, many
kinds are available year-round. These terms relate to the stages
of maturity at which they are harvested.

The so-called summer squash includes those which are harvested
while still immature, soft-skinned, and small. Because the skin
and seeds are eaten as well, they should be tender, fresh, and fairly
heavy in relation to their size. They should be refrigerated and
eaten as soon as possible.

The winter varieties are those which are marketed when fully mature. These are hard shelled and range from small to very large. Their shells, of course, should not have any softness that would indicate immaturity and thin flesh. Hard-shelled squash may be stored in a cool, dry room for a fairly long period.

SOFT-SKINNED SQUASH

Zucchini. Also called *vegetable* or *Italian marrow,* it is shaped like a long cucumber with a green skin and what looks like yellowish stripes; it may be 2 to 3 inches thick.

Patty Pan. Disk shaped, with scalloped edge, smooth pale green to white skin, best harvested when 3 to 4 inches across.

Yellow Crookneck. Has a curved neck, larger at top than at base, and warted, the skin is light yellow when young and deep yellow when mature; best harvested when light yellow and about 4 to 5 inches long.

Yellow Straightneck. This is the same as crookneck except it's much larger and can be as much as 20 inches long and 4 inches thick.

HARD-SHELLED SQUASH

Acorn. So-called because of its acorn-like shape, it is 6 to 8 inches long, 4 or 5 inches thick, with a smooth, dark green, ridged hard shell, which turns to orange during storage.

Butternut. Round, pear shaped and up to a foot long, these have a smooth, hard, light brown, or dark yellow skin.

Hubbard. Large, up to 12 inch diameter, quite round, with a hard and bumpy skin, they are either dark green, bluish gray or red orange in color.

Pumpkin. Also a squash, round or oval, they come in a variety of sizes from small as a grapefruit to the truly large Halloween size; they are generally used in the traditional pie rather than as a vegetable.

To prepare and cook: soft-skinned squash should be washed and scrubbed, with the stem and blossom ends removed. If they are very small, they can be left whole, but larger vegetables can be cut into ¾-inch slices. Cook covered in a few tablespoons of boiling salted water for 10 or 15 minutes, then uncover and boil rapidly until any liquid evaporates. Season to taste.

Hard-shelled squash is usually baked. Wash and cut into halves or, if very large, into serving size portions, and remove the seeds and stringy insides. Squash can be dotted with butter, seasoned with salt and pepper, and placed in a covered baking dish or wrapped in foil (unwrap during the last 15 minutes of baking). Squash also may be baked uncovered for 20 to 30 minutes if the cut side is put face downward on the pan. Winter squash takes from 30 to 60 minutes in a hot oven to become tender.

Sweet Potatoes

The sweet potato is not a potato but a vegetable that is native to the tropical part of our continent. It is actually a large root of the morning glory family. Two types of sweet potatoes are available in varying amounts throughout the year: the moist sweet type (sometimes incorrectly called yams) and the dry type. (The true yam is an entirely different plant and is not grown commercially in the United States.)

The moist type of sweet potatoes are the more widely marketed; they have deep yellow or orange red flesh and are very sweet. The dry type has a light-colored skin and after cooking has a light yellow flesh that is dry and somewhat grainy. Good sweet potatoes of either type should be well-shaped, smooth, and have uniformly colored skins that are free from signs of decay. Sweet potatoes are more perishable than white potatoes and should never be stored in the refrigerator as cold is harmful to them.

To prepare and cook: wash clean and cook with skins in covered pan of boiling salted water for about 25 to 35 minutes. Cool until potatoes can be handled, peel, and serve plain with butter and seasoning or mash.

Sweet potatoes are frequently baked. Lightly grease the sweet potatoes and bake 30 to 50 minutes. Serve as is or use in other dishes.

In some parts of the country, sweet potatoes are used instead of pumpkin for the traditional pie.

Tomatoes

Tomatoes technically are a fruit, but they're included under vegetables because that's the way everyone uses them.

Tomatoes marketed in cellophane cartons are a familiar consumer gripe. Fully-ripe tomatoes simply cannot be shipped over long distances, and during the October through June period they cannot be grown locally in most parts of the country. Tomatoes are picked green and shipped for arrival at the store in almost ripe condition. Most are grown in California, Florida, and Texas. As many of the cellophane cartons of tomatoes carry brand names, perhaps your best guide is to find a brand that you like and continue to buy this kind.

Beginning in June and July, most areas of the country have abundant supplies of locally grown tomatoes, which can be sold vine-ripened. There is a taste difference, so enjoy home-grown tomatoes during their season.

In general, try to select tomatoes that are well formed, smooth, and reasonably free from blemishes. In fully ripe fruit, look for an overall rich red color and a slight softness.

Tomatoes usually have better flavor and texture if you continue the ripening process at home by leaving them at room temperature for a day or two, or until they turn deep red. Then they may be kept in the refrigerator for some time, but store with care as tomatoes turn mushy if they get anywhere near freezing temperature.

Tomatoes are served in endless ways: raw in salads, sandwiches, and as a side vegetable; stewed, baked, broiled; used as an ingredient in a variety of dishes from casseroles to spaghetti sauces; and pickled or preserved. Check a cookbook for ideas.

Turnips and Rutabagas

There are various sizes and shapes among these root vegetables. The most popular type of turnips have white skins, which turn an attractive purple at the top, and white flesh. Early turnips are small and tender and may be cooked or eaten raw as an appetizer or salad ingredient. Late or main crop turnips are larger in size and come in a variety of shapes, but the different varieties have much the same flavor.

Rutabagas, sometimes known as Swedish turnips, are a large-sized relative of the turnip. They have smooth, yellowish skin and flesh that has a slightly sweet flavor. Late winter storage rutabagas are sometimes coated with a thin layer of wax or paraffin to prevent spoiling, and this should be removed.

In buying both vegetables, look for smooth, fairly firm vegetables, without skin punctures or obvious fibrous roots.

To cook: both turnips and rutabagas can be washed, pared, and sliced or diced, and cooked in a small amount of boiling salted water. Turnips should cook for 12 to 15 minutes, rutabagas for 25 to 40 minutes. Drain and season to taste. Very small turnips can be cooked whole.

Turnip tops, when fresh and tender, are eaten as a "green" (see the greens entry for tips on preparation).

Watercress and Parsley

Watercress is a small, round-leafed plant that grows along the banks of freshwater streams and ponds. It is on the market all year in small amounts. Parsley is a small, curly- or flat-leaved plant that grows well in any kitchen garden and is in good supply in the markets.

Both have dark green leaves and are good sources of vitamin A. They are used in salads and for garnishes. Both are sold in bunches. As with other greens, look for crisp, bright green leaves and avoid wilted or yellowed bunches. Both watercress and parsley should be washed several times in cold running water and kept cold and humid. Watercress is very perishable and should be used as soon as possible.

CHAPTER 5

The Bread and Cereal Group

Through the ages much of women's work, and men's work too, has been devoted to preserving foods for later use—smoking, drying, pickling, and, more recently, canning, freezing, and irradiating. In one important food, however, the process is reversed. We take grains, which are storable commodities, and turn them into perishable foods, such as breads, cereals, and crackers.

One of the four basic food groups, the bread and cereal group tends to be neglected by calorie-conscious adults. Four or more servings a day are recommended by the U.S. Department of Agriculture. A slice of bread, 1 ounce of ready-to-eat cereal, or ½ to ¾ cup of cooked cereal is defined as a serving, as is one-half cup of spaghetti, macaroni, noodles, or rice. Advice on how to buy the latter group is given in Chapter 7.

Bread

There is a wide range of variety and price in breads, and there are differences in their nutrition. With the exception of the black breads of Europe, which are pure rye, all breads we find in the supermarket and bakery contain some wheat, which provides the gluten that makes "rising" possible. Even the heavy pumpernickel is about 20 percent wheat flour. The other common rye breads, in ascending order of color, are light pumpernickel, Swedish sweet, Swedish sour, American, German, Bohemian, and Jewish. They contain differing amounts of dark rye flour, medium rye flour, or white rye flour, which are used in combination with wheat flour. Jewish rye, for instance, has 40 to 70 percent wheat flour, but its special flavor is due to the fact that it is the only major rye bread which calls for malt syrup in its formulation.

Another factor which influences taste is the type of leavening that is used. Yeast is the leavening agent used in most bread. It acts on the sugars and starches during fermentation to make bubbles in the stringy gluten. The sourdough process, which goes back to antiquity, uses a special "sour" starter or mixes some fermented or sour dough from a previous batch into the new dough. Even sourdoughs differ; the famous French sourdough of San Francisco has a different flavor from that of New Orleans.

Categorizing and describing breads is difficult because local custom and taste have brought about a wide variety of breads. Their names don't always identify the same products in different parts of the country. Only five types of bread have been given an official "standard of identity" by the Food and Drug Administration. These are white bread, enriched white bread, whole wheat bread, milk bread, and raisin bread. Even within these classifications, there are enough optional ingredients that breads with the same name can be significantly different in taste and texture and modestly different in nutrition.

Potato bread, buttermilk bread, or butter bread have relatively small amounts of extra ingredients—not enough to change the nutrition greatly, but enough to give a special flavor to what is essentially white bread.

Classic French bread is made of white flour, water, salt, and yeast, but without shortening and enrichment. Bakers can and do enrich some French bread and add shortening.

Despite these differences, breads, rolls, and buns are becoming more similar nutritionally, owing to the widening practice of enriching all bakery products. California and Arizona have laws which require any product composed of 25 percent or more flour to be enriched.

Here are some tips for knowledgeable buying of breads.

1. Buy by weight, not by size. Common sizes are 1-pound, 1½-pound, and 2-pound loaves. The big, soft loaf which is popular for children's sandwiches may look bigger but actually can be the same weight and nutritionally equivalent to a small, firm bread.

2. Look for markdowns on day-old, house brand baked goods. You won't find markdowns on national brands because bakers pick up day-old products at the stores and sell them in their own "thrift stores."

3. Look for the word "enriched" on the labels of white bread and hamburger and hot dog buns. Most are enriched, but remember the enriched white product has three times as much iron and vitamins as unenriched white bread. Whole wheat is about equal to enriched white bread in nutritional value, but rye and pumpernickel are lower in B vitamins and iron.

4. Buy the specials. Bread is often among the "advertised specials" and is offered at very good prices.

5. Investigate variety breads. Although they are usually more expensive than enriched white bread, they offer a change of pace and still represent excellent value for the money.

6. Buy only as much as you can use within a week. Mold retardants and antistaling additives in enriched white bread and rolls, whole wheat bread, and raisin bread will permit safe storage for that period.

7. If you buy French bread, Italian bread, "natural" bread,

rye, or pumpernickel, plan to use them that day or within 24 or 48 hours. French and Italian breads lose their fresh flavor quickly, and "natural" breads, which have no preservatives, will mold and stale quickly, as will rye and pumpernickel breads.

8. Consider another convenience product, refrigerated biscuits in a tube, which are a bargain at about a penny a piece and which lend themselves to many shortcut ways of preparing hors d'oeuvres or pastries. Check your cookbooks for ideas.

9. Remember the versatility of bread. Bread crumbs provide firmness in many meatball or meatloaf recipes, and making your own is cheaper than buying them. Toasted bread cubes can replace rice and noodles in many casserole recipes, again at a lower cost. Moistened bread pressed into muffin tins makes quick patty shells. So, buy enough to have on hand for these and other uses.

Bread should be stored at room temperature; refrigeration retards mold but speeds staling. Freezing does help and is a great aid in having just the right amount of bread on hand, but it is a luxury to give up valuable freezer space to such a bulky product.

Standards of Identity

For the past 20 years, bakers have operated under "standards of identity" for bread and bread-like rolls and buns. This means that in addition to flour, water, yeast and salt—the basic ingredients of any bread—only certain approved additional ingredients may be used, and some of these have limitations on amount. There are over 100 of these optional ingredients, one of which is *spice,* a term covering quite a few specific ingredients. In actual practice, a baker might use only a half-dozen of these additives in a particular type of bread. He would, for instance, probably use only one of the 22 approved forms of milk and buttermilk: milk, concentrated milk, evaporated milk, dried, skim, concentrated skim, and so on. He would probably use only one of the mold retardants and only one of the antistaling agents. In the case of enriched bread, he would also use enriched flour or put the four enrichment ingredients directly in the dough.

The standard of identity for raisin bread calls for the same general ingredients as white bread plus a minimum of 50 parts by weight of seeded or seedless raisins for each 100 parts by weight of flour. It works out that you get about 3 to 4 ounces of raisins in the pound of raisin bread. This bread also may be iced or frosted.

The standard for milk bread requires that milk, or its equivalent in a reconstitutable ingredient like evaporated skim milk, be used instead of water as the moistening ingredient in preparing the dough. The standard for whole wheat states, not surprisingly, that there can be no flour content other than whole wheat flour. The same applies to *graham bread* and *entire wheat bread*, which are synonymous with *whole wheat bread*. It does not apply, however, to *wheat bread*, which may be any combination of whole wheat and white flours. But wheat bread is not a standardized product; consequently, its label must list ingredients in order of weight. The standard of identity for white bread permits up to 3 percent corn flour (or rice flour, sweet potato starch, or several other such ingredients), and no label declaration is required. If the baker wants to produce a delicious corn-rye bread, he must identify it and list the ingredients on the label.

Have you ever wondered about the difference between bread and rolls? The official difference is simply size. The FDA standards of identity require that the bread be baked "in units, each of which weighs one-half pound or more after cooling"; rolls and buns weigh less than one-half pound each.

Enrichment

Many foods are "fortified" with different nutrients which upgrade the product generally. "Enrichment," the addition of iron and three B vitamins, thiamin, niacin, and riboflavin, was inaugurated in 1941 for the specific purpose of combatting the nutritional deficiency diseases known as beriberi, pellagra, ariboflavinosis, and iron deficiency anemia. For many years it was applied only to white bread, bread-type rolls and buns, and white flour. Recently, however, bakers have been enriching a long list of breads, rolls, pies, cakes, crackers, and cookies. Noodles and macaroni products are being enriched, and the process can logically be extended to any wheat product.

The Price of Convenience in the Bakery Department

Comparisons, based on prices in Washington, D.C. in March 1972, showed these differences among various ways of buying bread or ingredients.

Cost for one-pound loaf or equivalent

"Made from scratch" homemade bread	25¢
Refrigerated biscuits	23¢
Dry biscuit mix, including milk	20¢
Regular enriched white bread	25–30¢
Frozen bread (to be baked)	20–30¢
Brown-and-serve bread	47¢

Here are comparisons of five different ways of buying pumpkin pie.

Pies (6 servings per pie)

	Cost per serving
Frozen (allow hour for baking)	16.5¢
Canned pie filling plus crust from a mix	12.0¢
"Made from scratch" with canned pumpkin	12.0¢
House brand pie in supermarket	12.5¢
Retail bakery pie	15.0¢

Breakfast Cereals, Hot or Cold

In buying cereals, storage space, rate of use, nutritional attributes, convenience, and desire for variety are factors to weigh against prices.

Among the oatmeals priced in the Washington, D.C. area, the individual preflavored packets came to 80¢ per pound, national brand "old-fashioned" oats cost 31¢ per pound, a large (42-ounce) box of quick-cooking oats cost 25¢ per pound, and a house brand large size of quick-cooking oats was lowest at 22¢ per pound.

Below are some sample prices which illustrate the differences in price per pound for various size packages of a popular brand of corn flakes:

Size	Price per package	Price per pound
Corn flakes		
8-pack, 8 ounce	38¢	76¢
regular 8 ounce	22¢	44¢
12 ounce	29¢	39¢
18 ounce	39¢	35¢
Presugared corn flakes		
10 ounce	39¢	62¢
15 ounce	52¢	55¢

The price per pound for the 8-pack is quite high. However, if cold cereal is not eaten regularly, the large package will probably become stale before it is used.

CHAPTER 6

What Price Convenience?

Even if you're a gourmet cook who likes to work from basic ingredients, there will be times when you will want to take advantage of the savings in time and trouble provided by convenience foods. Although convenience foods usually will cost more than their home-prepared counterparts, some actually cost less or just a few pennies more.

This chapter will offer you guidelines for purchasing canned foods, frozen foods, and convenience foods in cardboard cartons. Many of these guidelines have already been mentioned in the discussions of the meat, dairy, produce, and bakery departments.

Canned Foods

Canned foods almost deserve a chapter of their own because they constitute such a large part of our food purchases. You carry home about 500 cans a year, making a total annual U.S. consumption of 27 billion jars and cans of food.

Here are some pointers about buying canned foods:

1. Take advantage of sales to build a modest reserve supply of canned goods, in addition to your "emergency shelf" supplies. Especially watch for items you use regularly as staples: canned tomatoes, evaporated milk, tuna, and so on.

2. Select a can size appropriate for your needs. Use the can size chart that follows as a guide to how many cups per can size you can count on.

3. Choose the quality you need. For example, canned tomato wedges are fine for wintertime salads, but if you are simply going to toss the tomatoes into a casserole, they may be 50 percent more expensive than low-priced stewed tomatoes, which are just as nutritious and palatable.

CANNED FOODS SIZE CHART

The *8 ounce* jar or can is equivalent to approximately *1 cup*.

This size is often referred to as the "buffet" size and is used principally for fruits, vegetables, and special food combinations for small families. (2 servings)

The *10½ to 12 ounce* can yields about *1¼ cups*.

Sometimes called the "picnic can," this size is used primarily for condensed soups, some fruits, vegetables, meats, fish, and food combination "specialties." (2 to 3 servings)

The *12 ounce* (vac.) can yields about *1½ cups*.

Principally for vacuum pack corn, this has three to four servings.

The *14 to 16 ounce* can (No. 300) yields *1¾ cups*.

Commonly called the "1 pound" can, it is used for pork and beans, baked beans, meat products, cranberry sauce, blueberries, and specialties. (3 to 4 servings)

The *16 to 17 ounce* can (No. 303) yields *2 cups*.

Often called the "16 or 17 ounce" can or jar, it is the principal size used for fruits and vegetables, some meat products, ready-to-serve soups, and specialties. (4 servings)

The *20 ounce* (1 lb., 4 oz.) or *18 fl. ounce* (1 pt., 2 fl. oz.) can (No. 2) yields *2½ cups.*

This is used for juices, ready-to-serve soups, some specialties, pineapple, and apple slices; it is no longer in popular use for most fruits and vegetables. (5 servings)

The *27 to 29 ounce* (1 lb., 11 oz. to 1 lb., 13 oz.) can or jar (No. 2½) yields *3½ cups.*

This size is used for fruits and some vegetables, (pumpkin, sauerkraut, spinach and other greens, tomatoes). (5 to 7 servings)

The *51 ounce* (3 lb., 3 oz.) or *46 fl. ounce* (1 qt., 14 fl. oz.) yields *5¾ cups.*

This size can is used for fruit and vegetable juices, pork and beans, institutional size for condensed soups, and some vegetables. (10 to 12 servings)

4. Read the labels. The weight or capacity of the can (and *can* includes the glass jar) is required by law to be included on every label. Price comparisons are much easier now with unit pricing, which can give you the per-ounce or per-quart price of two or more competing products. Labels also show the ingredients of combination foods, listed in order of their predominance.

5. A variety of canned soups, so handy for quick lunches and snacks, can provide the base for a whole range of sauces for vegetables. They can also be used in casseroles. Competing with the familiar condensed soups are the full-strength luncheon soups (consider the cost per serving as well as the taste) and the dried soups (which may be the best per-serving buy). The new instant (make it in a cup) soups are convenient for the solitary luncher but are correspondingly more expensive.

6. Provide orderly storage for canned goods. A large part of their value is storability, but this requires adequate space. If you are cramped for space in a small house or apartment, add a shelf or two to part of a closet or arrange some cartons in whatever area you can. The storage space should be warm but not hot, and canned and bottled goods should not be permitted to freeze. Canned foods have lengthy shelf life, but keep moving the older cans out front so you'll use them first.

7. As to canned food safety, a simple rule is never to use bloated or leaking cans. Throw them out immediately and place out of reach of any pets. Slightly rusted cans or slightly dented cans are all right. Your chances of being stricken with serious illness through

food poisoning from canned goods is remote, but don't take chances with suspicious cans. If you notice you have somehow brought home a bad-looking can, return it to the store and it will be replaced.

Freshness in the Frozen Food Case

Frozen fruits and vegetables are as "fresh" as the fruits and vegetables you buy in the produce department and thus are nutritionally as valuable. They are picked at the peak of their ripeness and processed and packaged almost immediately.

Frozen foods will lose their freshness if they're not promptly put into your home freezer. That's why it's a good rule to select frozen foods last. Storage should be in a freezer which maintains 0° F. The ice cube compartment of a refrigerator is not cold enough for storing frozen foods.

Frozen foods are already washed, pared, chopped, diced, mashed, or sliced, making them very convenient. The "no waste" character of frozen fruits and vegetables means that they're generally lower in cost than their fresh counterparts, except when the fresh foods are at the peak of their season.

Most stores offer plain frozen fruits and vegetables in either 9-ounce or 10-ounce cartons or large 1¾-pound or 2-pound poly bags. In house brands, the price difference between the two is actually very minor, usually only tenths of a cent per ounce. Poly bags are likely to offer savings when compared with small cartons of national brands. Their main advantage is that you can pour out enough for one serving or eight. Many one, two, and five person families find the 10-ounce carton too restrictive, and if they have the freezer space, they prefer the poly bags.

Frozen french fries in the 2-pound poly bags are actually 2 cents a serving cheaper than making them yourself, according to U.S. Department of Agriculture figures compiled in June 1971. Frozen french fries in the small 9-ounce carton are even a little cheaper than homemade, and that's without putting any value on the time and skill required to turn out good french fries in the kitchen. A still greater bargain in potatoes is dehydrated mashed potatoes, which the USDA priced at 2.9 cents per serving if bought in the 2-pound package, compared with 4.3 cents for french fries in the 2-pound package. More expensive are dehydrated au gratin potatoes which cost 3 cents a serving more than making them from scratch.

Frozen juices are real convenience food bargains, especially if you can use the larger-size cans. Frozen orange concentrate actually is the lowest cost way to buy orange juice. The U.S. Department of Agriculture June 1971 study shows the following costs per serving:

Orange Juice	Price per market unit	Servings per unit	Cost per 1/2 cup serving	Cost relative to cost of home-squeezed juice
	Cents	Number	Cents	Percent
Home squeezed, 5 pounds oranges used	78	8.6	9.1	100
Fresh, store squeezed, 32 fluid ounce container	44	8.0	5.5	60
Canned juice:				
18 fluid ounce can	19	4.5	4.3	47
46 fluid ounce can	46	11.5	4.0	44
Frozen concentrate:				
6 fluid ounce can	24	6.2	4.0	44
12 fluid ounce can	46	12.4	3.7	41
16 fluid ounce can	60	16.6	3.7	41

"What price convenience" becomes a more important question when you start to deal with the endless new combinations of vegetables—creamed, sauced, with baby onions, with mushrooms, with almonds—now available both in cartons and boil-in-the-bags. For these you definitely pay for the convenience, and you must decide whether it's worth it.

Frozen pizza, lasagna, and ravioli, as well as the growing variety of frozen Chinese foods, rate consideration, too, because they're only a little more expensive than their homemade counterparts. Frozen chicken chow mein is, in fact, cheaper, and canned chow mein is the cheapest of all. These dishes are time consuming to prepare at home and require a variety of ingredients, which are not always readily at hand.

All kinds of breakfast items can be found in the frozen food case, with frozen waffles being one of the newest and most popular. At about a nickel each, they're more expensive than making them yourself from scratch or from a mix.

Frozen biscuits and frozen pies and cakes are other offerings that are more expensive than home-prepared and usually are more expensive than those made from a mix. Not in the frozen food case, but in the refrigerated dairy case, are the biscuits in the can that you bake in the oven. You literally can't make them yourself more cheaply. If you buy to keep them on hand, watch the date code to be sure you use them on time.

Convenience in Cardboard or Foil

An excellent illustration of the mixed emotions we all have about using the convenience foods now on the market is the experience of a leading manufacturer of cake mixes. When they first developed a cake mix that required only the addition of water, thus freeing women from the bother and uncertainty of mixing a cake, they expected to be rewarded with booming sales. On the contrary, these first cake mixes sold poorly. Consumer research showed that women really didn't want to have everything done for them. So, the manufacturer reformulated the mix to make it necessary to add eggs, as well as water, and sales did boom.

We've come a long way since then. Pie crust mix, cake mix, and biscuit mix are so widely accepted now that many people think that pies, cakes, and biscuits made from a mix are home-made. Because they're sold in such large volume, we are paying practically no premium for the convenience, and the quality and flavor are excellent.

Cake frosting mixes are more expensive than those you prepare yourself, but their almost absolute dependability and delicious flavor and appearance may make them well worth the money.

Among the relative newcomers on the market are the 20 to 30 variations of seasoned rice and seasoned macaroni. However, the seasoned versions are fairly expensive, and it generally seems worthwhile to add your own seasonings. Prices for the seasoned varieties are 5 to 7 cents an ounce because they usually come in small packages. But if you can use a 2-pound package of rice, it'll cost just over a penny an ounce for long-grain rice or about 2 cents an ounce for enriched parboiled rice, a product which is high in nutrition. (See Chapter 7 on beans, rice, and pasta.)

If you don't trust your own seasoning ability or dislike measuring minute quantities of this and that, you'll do slightly better with the foil-wrapped packets of mix, which are discussed below. At 20 to 25 cents a packet, you can get enough seasoning for 8 ounces of rice.

Still another variation are the packages of seasoned rice, seasoned potatoes, and seasoned macaroni and spaghetti, to which you add a pound of meat. Usually you can do as well with a good cookbook, the basic ingredients, a well stocked herb shelf, and a little more time. Just be sure when you're comparing prices that you add the cost of the pound of beef.

Extremely useful are the foil-wrapped packages of dip mix, salad dressing mix, gravy mix, and sauce mix. Many of them are interchangeable in an emergency. Salad dressing mix can easily become dip mix, and dip mix can be turned into sauce mix. See the chapter on shortenings, oils, and salad dressings for more on the economics of salad dressing mixes.

"Convenience" means many different things. There's convenience in size, in premeasured ingredients, and in eliminating messy, time-consuming steps in the kitchen. There's convenience in a dependable recipe the inexperienced cook can trust, in having shortcuts available for emergencies, and in the year-round availability of out-of-season products. Some convenience really isn't more expensive, chiefly because the product is so widely accepted and, therefore, manufactured or processed in such large volumes that it can be sold at bargain prices. Much of it is more expensive, though, and you will have to make your own decisions about how much it's worth to you.

CHAPTER 7

Dried Beans, Rice, Pastas

Perhaps more than any other products, dried beans, rice, and pasta can lend themselves to filling, nutritious meals at bargain prices.

Beans

The bean is one of the most hearty, versatile, and healthful foods available. Dried beans, peas, and lentils contain so much protein that they are considered part of the meat group in the basic four food groups. They are recognized as a meat substitute, not only for their protein, but for their vitamins, iron, and food energy as well. A cup of cooked or 3-ounces of dried beans satisfies the requirement of one of the two servings a day you need from the meat group if you serve them with, or combine them with, milk or cheese.

Beans also can't be beaten for versatility and convenience. Limas, navy beans, lentils, white or red kidney beans, split peas, and blackeye peas each have a different taste, and a host of different recipes can be used to vary them pleasantly. You'll find them on the supermarket shelves at about the same price all year round, and at home they'll store almost indefinitely with a few simple precautions. In the see-through bag or cardboard box they're fine as long as you keep them in a cool, dry place. Once you open them, put them in a glass or metal jar or some other container with a tight-fitting lid. Don't mix the contents of packages bought at different times, particularly if they were purchased several months apart. Older beans usually take longer to cook than fresher ones.

Beans are cheap enough to enable you to buy more than one kind and still economize. A pound of beans of almost any variety may still be bought for as little as 20 cents a pound, which means you can serve your family a cup of beans for 5 to 7 cents a serving. This compares favorably with 1964 prices, when beans were about 15 cents a pound. Dry beans are a food that seems to be less affected by inflation than others.

Not all varieties of dried beans will be found in all parts of the country, so check your supermarket shelves to see what is most popular in your area. In the West there are more red beans and pintos for Mexican dishes, whereas in New England you'll find pea and navy beans favored for baking. There are always many popular varieties to choose from, wherever you live. Here's a list of the most common beans.

Black beans. These are used in thick soups and in Oriental and Mediterranean dishes.

Blackeye peas. This Southern favorite is actually a bean but has different names in different parts of the country. Sometimes they are called "cow peas." Small, oval-shaped, and creamy white with a black spot on one side, they are used primarily as a main dish vegetable.

Garbanzo beans. More generally known as *chick peas*, they are nut flavored and often are pickled in vinegar and oil for salads. They can also be used as a main dish vegetable in the unpickled form. Similar beans are *cranberry* and *yellow-eye* beans.

Great Northern beans. Medium-sized, oval, and white, these beans are used in soups, salads, casserole dishes, and home-baked beans.

Kidney beans. Large, red or white in color, and kidney-shaped. they are popular for chili con carne and add zest to salads and many Mexican dishes.

Lima beans. Broad and flat, they come in different sizes, but size does not affect quality. They make an excellent main dish vegetable and can be used in casseroles.

Navy beans. This category includes *Great Northern, pea, flat small white*, and *small white beans*.

Pea beans. Small, oval, and white, these are a favorite for home-baked beans, soups, and casseroles. They hold their shape even when cooked until tender.

Pinto beans. In the same family as kidney and red beans, beige-colored and speckled, they are used mainly in salads and chili.

Red and pink beans. Used in many Mexican dishes and chili, they are related to the kidney bean.

Dry peas. These may be green or yellow, but the green type has a more distinctive flavor. They are available either whole or split and are used to make soups, casseroles, vegetable side dishes, dips, and hors d'oeuvres. *Dry split peas* have had their skins removed and are mainly used for soup. Green and yellow whole peas and green and yellow split peas, even though they may vary in taste a little, are used interchangeably in many recipes.

Some experts insist on soaking dried beans, while others say it isn't necessary. Both ways give good results. All you have to remember is that beans that are not soaked take a little longer to cook. Boil them for two minutes first, if you want to soak for only an hour, or soak overnight, whichever is more convenient. If you have any doubts about which method to use, check the instructions on the package.

Remember to make allowances for the increased volume of dried beans. One cup of dried beans usually makes 2 or 3 cups after cooking, depending on the variety. Also, add salt and acid ingredients, such as tomatoes, catsup, or vinegar, near the end of the cooking time. Acids and salt prevent beans and peas from softening.

Rice

It's no accident that rice is a staple for so much of the world's population. It's inexpensive, nutritious, and easy to cook. It can be boiled, steamed, oven-cooked, or fried. Costing as little as 6 cents for a 1-cup serving, it is a good budget item.

An important thing to remember is that most kinds of rice will swell considerably during cooking. One cup of raw rice will turn into 2 cups or more of cooked rice, and the various other types of rice also will swell in varying degrees.

Long grain rice is fluffy, dry, and firm but tender, with each grain separate. The short grain or medium grain rice is moist, and the grains tend to cling together. Some people prefer this. Such rice is also good to use in patties and croquettes. On the whole, long grain is a bit more expensive than short grain.

Of course, it is more economical to buy plain, natural rice that hasn't been processed in any way. Today many people are buying a processed variety which is *parboiled*. Parboiled rice has undergone special steam pressure before milling that forces the vitamins and minerals from the hull, bran, and germ into the starchy portion. This rice, which is usually enriched to give it more nutrition, takes slightly longer to cook than regular rice. Because it is the long-grained variety, the cooked grains are fluffy, separate, and plump.

Precooked rice, known as *instant* rice, is also the enriched, long-grained variety and will yield 1 to 2 cups of cooked rice for 1 cup of uncooked rice.

Other kinds of rice will dress up a meal or make a recipe unique. Brown rice has a nutlike flavor, a slightly chewy consistency, and needs a bit longer cooking time than regular white rice. It's a whole grain rice from which only a small amount of bran has been removed. The oil in the bran reduces its shelf life (it gets a rancid flavor), and because it is handled in much smaller volume, it is usually more costly. But it gives variety to your menu, and if brown rice continues to grow in popularity, it could become even less expensive than white rice.

Wild rice is not a true rice; it is the seed of a grass that grows wild in shallow lakes and marshes. It is much more expensive than any of the regular types of rice because it must be harvested by hand from boats. But it is considered a gourmet dish by many and can add an elegant flair to a company meal. To cut down on the rather strong flavor, and also to stretch dollars, wild rice can be mixed with regular white rice.

Consider, too, the many seasoned rices that are available today —beef, chicken, chili, cheese, curry, and herb. Also available now are frozen rice pilaf and canned Spanish rice, as well as many other specialties. These are fairly expensive. See Chapter 6 for more information.

A few cooking hints may be helpful. It is not necessary to wash rice before cooking. Rice is clean as it comes from the package, and washing just wastes valuable minerals and vitamins. The same goes for rinsing after cooking. Be careful to follow package directions and add exactly the amount of water the rice will absorb during cooking. Too much water makes the rice sticky and gummy.

Leftover cooked rice can be added to many dishes that call for a starchy food, for example, soups, stews, and casseroles. Also, many fruit and gelatin desserts call for cooked rice.

Pasta

Pasta is the generic term for more than a hundred different shapes of macaroni products, broadly grouped into three main categories: spaghetti, macaroni, and noodles. Spaghettini is thinner than regular spaghetti, and vermicelli is thinnest of all. Short curved spaghetti is also available, and there are small- and jumbo-sized macaroni shells and noodle bows. Noodles come in widths from fine to broad, including the very broad lasagna or pot pie type. There are dozens of other unusual forms, many with exotic Italian names, such as manicotti, rigatoni, green noodles (that contain spinach), and cresta di gallo (shaped like a rooster's crest).

You may also wish to keep a selection of the many types of canned, packaged, or frozen pasta on hand for quick snacks or last-minute dinners.

Pasta is made from durum wheat, a hard wheat with a high gluten content and a yellowish color. In milling durum wheat, the bran and germ are removed and the starchy inner portion is ground coarsely to produce semolina. The semolina is then mixed to a stiff dough with water and forced through a die that shapes it.

To make it more nutritious, the ground wheat flour, or semolina, is enriched, so in macaroni products you have another low-priced variety of food items that are nutritious as well as good-tasting. Pasta products seldom vary in price and are invaluable in making your meals go further. They combine well with meat, fish, poultry, cheese, and eggs and can be the basis for a main dish or a side dish or incorporated into salads, soups, or hors d'oeuvres.

The basic method for cooking macaroni products calls for a large pot, rapidly boiling water, and short cooking times, usually from 8 to 10 minutes. Add a tablespoon of oil per quart of water to keep the pasta separated and to keep it from sticking to the pot.

Generally speaking, noodles will yield about the same amount cooked as uncooked, but elbow macaroni and spaghetti will double in volume when cooked; so make the necessary allowances.

Pasta products, like rice and dried beans, should be kept in a cool, dry place. After opening the packages, place the contents in a container with a tightly fitted lid. (A seald plastic bag will also do.)

Other Grains

Bulgur

A good example of a peasant food that is finding its way into gourmet cookery, bulgur is prized for its hearty nut-like flavor. Bulgur is simply wheat that is parboiled to help pop off some of the bran and crack the kernels, then dried to improve storability. Because of this precooking, it can be prepared by the methods used for cooking rice and may be used in many of the same recipes.

Corn Meal

Made from both white and yellow varieties of corn, white corn meal is favored in the southern United States, and yellow in the northern states. The two are interchangeable in recipes, but the yellow corn meal has higher vitamin A value. Corn meal is used for baking cornbreads, spoonbreads (a southern variation made with white corn meal), and other quickbreads and muffins. It is also served as a hot cereal, long known as *mush,* and the cooked mush can be chilled and then sliced, fried, and eaten with syrup.

Hominy

This is to corn what bulgur is to wheat. Generally made from white corn, the hull and germ are removed from the whole kernels, either by soaking in lye or by machinery. Hominy may be cooked in milk or water and served as a vegetable. Because of relatively low demand, some stores may not regularly stock hominy or may offer only a canned variety. Nevertheless, it is a good food that can add variety to your table.

Hominy grits are ground hominy which cooks to the consistency of a hot breakfast cereal. In the South grits are regularly served as an accompaniment to eggs and bacon. Grits also can be prepared as a casserole with cheese to serve in place of potatoes or rice.

CHAPTER 8

Shortenings, Oils, and Salad Dressings

Fats and oils contain fatty acids that are essential to good nutrition—in moderation, of course. Furthermore, we depend on them to do three important things for us in cooking:

1. To give richness and flavor, as when butter or margarine are added to vegetables or oil is used in salad dressing.

2. To fry foods. The choice of fats depends upon the flavor desired and the temperature to which fat will be heated. Bacon fat is popular for frying potatoes, but the flavor would tend to overpower many other foods which are sautéed or pan fried. Butter or margarine is popular for these, but butter will brown less readily than margarine if longer sautéing or pan frying is indicated.

Vegetable oils or hydrogenated shortenings work best for deep-fat frying because they can be heated to a high smoking point without changing composition and may be used when a distinct flavor is not desired.

3. To shorten, that is tenderize, baked foods such as cakes, pies, or biscuits. Any shortening or oil may be used, but one type should not be substituted for another without knowing the rules of substitution. These rules will be given later in this chapter.

Shortenings and Oils

For many years, *lard*, a pure white substance made from pork fat, was the all-purpose shortening, and some homemakers today still prefer it for flaky pie crusts and biscuits. Some lard must be refrigerated, so check the label. *Solid* hydrogenated vegetable fat shortenings later appeared on the market in convenient size cans. Because of the hydrogenation, they can be kept at room temperature without loss of quality for long periods of time.

Because fewer people today prepare pie crusts or other pastries from scratch, lard and hydrogenated shortening are not greatly in demand. We generally rely on one *oil* or *vegetable oil* for both cooking and salad dressing. Made from a variety of vegetable seeds, most of the commercial oils come from safflower seed, corn, soybean, cottonseed, olive, or peanut bases. Olive oil is the only one which is not recommended as an all-purpose oil, both because it's too expensive for cooking and because it tends to spatter when it's hot. However, its delicate flavor is highly regarded for salad dressing.

When buying all-purpose oils, select the largest size you can conveniently store and use it within a period of one to two months. Oils do get rancid, so store in a cool, dry place where they are not exposed to light. Unless you have a personal preference for peanut, corn, or safflower oil, shop for the lowest-cost product because "use" qualities are fairly similar.

Because oil adds more liquid and because there is a difference in "shortening power" among butter, margarine, lard, and hydrogenated fat, it may be risky to substitute in recipes which specify a particular type of shortening. If you have to substitute, these rules of thumb may help.

1. Lard has more shortening power than hydrogenated fat. Use only about ⅓ cup lard to 1 cup flour for pastry and 3 tablespoons lard to 1 cup of flour for biscuits.

2. If you are substituting hydrogenated shortening for butter, use 1 cup minus 2 tablespoons of hydrogenated shortening if recipe calls for 1 cup butter. If substituting butter or margarine for hydrogenated shortening, use 1 cup plus 2 tablespoons if recipe calls for 1 cup.

3. If substituting vegetable oil for one cup of melted butter or margarine in baking, use ⅞ cup oil plus ½ teaspoon of salt (the salt is needed to compensate for the seasoning that is lost by this substitution).

Salad Dressings

All salad dressings, including mayonnaise, can be made at home, but many people have come to appreciate the convenience of the premixed dressings in a bottle and the dressing mixes in a packet, which are simply combined with oil and vinegar, shaken, and served.

Few people bother making mayonnaise because it takes time to add the oil to the egg mixture. Instead they buy the ready-made kind. The product labeled salad dressing, which looks like mayonnaise, is several cents cheaper in the 8-ounce size and offers corresponding savings in larger sizes. Both mayonnaise and salad dressing contain eggs, but salad dressing includes a cooked starch paste, which is substituted for part of the egg, thus reducing the amount of oil that is added. Government standards require that mayonnaise contain a minimum of 65 percent oil by weight, while salad dressing must contain a minimum of 30 percent. You may find salad dressing perfectly satisfactory for spreading on bread for sandwiches and for fruit salads, but you may prefer the mayonnaise for potato salad because the oil and egg enhance the flavor.

Salad dressing is the obvious choice over mayonnaise if a lower-fat product is sought, although anyone on a low-fat diet probably should avoid both.

The most natural sources of animal fat—egg yolks, butterfat, and meat—are a combination of saturated, monounsaturated, and polyunsaturated fats, with a strong emphasis on the saturated fats. With the major exception of coconut oil, which is strongly saturated, the vegetable sources lean toward polyunsaturated, with safflower oil and corn oil at the top of the list of those in common use.

French dressing is a standardized product which must contain a minimum of 35 percent vegetable oil, but the variety of optional ingredients permitted makes it possible for manufacturers to develop their own recipes which have highly individual characteristics. French dressing made at home uses a ratio of ⅔ cup oil to 3 tablespoons of vinegar or lemon juice, with salt, pepper, and mustard flavoring. For a sweet version, 1 tablespoon of sugar may be added. Such homemade dressing comes to a total cost of about 20 to 25 cents for 8 ounces, depending on the quantities in which you purchased the original ingredients. The already prepared French dressings will range in price from 34 to 39 cents for 8 ounces; if you buy the 16-ounce size, prices would drop to 26 to 30 cents for 8 ounces.

Salad mixes in a packet cost about 20 cents each, and because you add your own oil and vinegar or lemon juice, another 12 to 15 cents must be added to the final cost of 8 ounces for comparison purposes.

CHAPTER 9

Beverages

Beverages, with the exception of milk and fruit juices, are purchased more for refreshment than nutrition. Here your selection is guided mainly by your personal preferences and your budget.

Coffee, Tea, and Cocoa

Coffee

Because all coffees are a blend, the various brands differ to some degree in aroma and flavor. Price isn't necessarily a guide here because you may find a brand which is relatively inexpensive but has the taste you like.

Select the grind you need for the brewing method you'll be using. Regular grind is used for steeped or percolator coffee, drip grind for drip coffee, and fine grind for vacuum coffee.

Because freshly ground or vacuum-packed coffee has better flavor, buy only as much as you can use in a week or so. A pound of regular coffee yields 40 cups. The 2-pound can may be a bargain, but it's not if it goes stale before you can use it. Store in an air-tight container once the can has been opened or you've brought a freshly ground bag home from the store. Keeping coffee in the refrigerator will help keep the flavor fresh and retard staling.

There's no reason, however, to pass up specials on vacuum-packed coffee because it will keep for a year as long as it's unopened.

Instant coffee has risen in popularity since World War II. It now accounts for more than one-quarter of all the cups of coffee drunk in the United States each year. Surprisingly, instant coffee is now cheaper than regular coffee and has the added advantage of being easier to keep fresh. Buy the larger size if you can use it in a reasonable length of time. The 6-ounce jar costs only about twice as much as the 2-ounce jar and will give you three times as many cups of coffee. Count on about 30 servings for each two ounces of instant.

Freeze-dried instants are more expensive, but because you use less they are worth consideration, particularly if the difference in flavor is important to you.

Decaffeinated coffee, as its name implies, is pure coffee from which almost all the caffeine has been removed.

Tea

Unlike coffee, the convenience forms of tea (tea bags and instant teas) are more expensive than regular tea leaves. A pound of tea will give you 200 cups, so tea bags may cost half again or twice as much. However, the ease of brewing a cup at a time and the convenience of the instants or the bags is more important to some people than the slight difference in cost per cup.

On the other hand, real tea lovers wouldn't trade properly brewed fresh tea for any number of tea bags or elaborately flavored instants. In all, there are more than 3,000 varieties of tea, which fall into three general classifications: *black*, *green*, and *oolong*. All three types come from the same tea bushes. It's what happens after the leaves are picked that makes them different.

Black tea undergoes a special processing treatment, oxidation, that turns the leaves black. In making green tea, the oxidation process is omitted. As a result, the tea is green in appearance and has a light color when brewed. Oolong tea is a compromise between black and green tea. It's semi-processed so the leaves are partly brown and partly green. It, too, brews light in color.

About 97 percent of all tea consumed in America is the black type. Tea terminology can be confusing because one set of names refers to the size of the leaves and another to the variety. Much of the tea you see in the store is labeled *orange pekoe* which is a size rather than a variety.

Most teas, like coffee, are blends. To help you find your way through the terminology in black teas, here's a guide from the Tea Council of America:

GRADES (SIZES) OF BLACK TEA

Orange Pekoe. Long, thin, wiry leaves which sometimes contain yellow tip or bud leaf. The liquors are light or pale in color.

Pekoe. The leaves of this grade are shorter and not so wiry as orange pekoe but the liquors generally have more color.

Souchong. A bold and round leaf, with pale liquors.

Broken Orange Pekoe. Much smaller than any of the leaf grades and usually contains yellow tip. The liquors have good color and strength in the cup and are the mainstay of a blend.

Broken Pekoe. Slightly larger than broken orange pekoe with rather less color in the cup; useful as a filler in a blend.

Broken Pekoe Souchong. A little larger or bolder than broken pekoe and in consequence lighter in the cup, but also used as a filler.

Fannings. Much smaller than broken orange pekoe and its main virtues are quick brewing with good color in the cup.

Dust. It is the name for the smallest grade produced. Very useful for a quick brewing, strong cup of tea; used only in blends of similar sized leaf, generally for catering purposes.

VARIETIES OF BLACK TEAS

Assam. A high grade India tea, grown in Assam Province in Northeast India. It makes a full-bodied, robust brew.

Ceylon. The best quality Ceylon teas are called *High Grown,* indicating teas grown at an elevation of more than 4,000 feet. Delicate and fragrant. Teas from the district of Uva are considered particularly fine.

Darjeeling. The finest and most delicately flavored of the India teas. Grown in the Himalaya Mountains at high elevations. Excellent flavor and aroma.

Earl Grey. Black tea from India and Ceylon. Makes an aromatic, hearty brew.

English Breakfast. A blend of black teas. Mellow and fragrant. Originally the name applied to China Congou teas; now it is used for blends of black teas in which the China character predominates.

Keemun. A fine grade tea of the China Congou type. Mild yet robust.

Lapsang Souchong. A tea with a unique smoky flavor. Originally a black China tea, this is now produced in Formosa. Pungent and strong.

GREEN TEAS

Basket Fired. A Japan tea that makes a light, gentle brew.

Gunpowder. A type of green tea from India, Ceylon, or Formosa in which each leaf is rolled into a small pellet. A delicate pale tea.

OOLONG AND MIXED TEAS

Formosa Oolong. A semi-fermented tea with subtle flavor and bouquet.

Jasmine. A delicately flavored tea, scented with white Jasmine blossoms.

Chocolate and Cocoa

Chocolate has probably been the single most successful inducement for children to drink milk. The bitter or baking chocolate we see in stores is simply the cleaned, roasted, and ground cocoa bean.

Sweet chocolate is made by adding sugar and flavorings to bitter chocolate and milk chocolate by adding milk as well. Bitter chocolate contains 50 to 58 percent of a fat called cocoa butter. Cocoa butter is extracted when chocolate is to be made into cocoa.

Breakfast or high-fat cocoa contains at least 22 percent fat, medium-fat cocoa contains 10 to 22 percent, and low-fat cocoa contains less than 10 percent. Dutch or Dutch-process cocoa is made by treating chocolate with alkali. The result is a darker but milder beverage.

Many people prefer cocoa to chocolate for making hot beverages. Its lower fat content makes it less likely to separate and it keeps better in hot weather. Also, it costs less.

Fruit Juices, Ades, and Drinks

Fruit juices, whether homemade, canned, frozen, or dehydrated, are a refreshing drink and provide you with vitamin C. Citrus juice and tomato juice are excellent natural sources of vitamin C. Most of the other common juices, pineapple, apple, grape, cranberry, are fair to poor sources. However, most of them on the market today are fortified with vitamin C or combined with citrus juices. Apricot nectar is a good source of vitamin A.

Reading labels before buying juices and juice drinks is important. To help end the confusion over terminology in the orange beverage field, the Food and Drug Administration, at the request of the citrus industry, established new standards effective in September 1972, requiring the percentage of orange juice to be stated prominently on the label:

Orange Juice Drink Blend Containing ___ percent Orange Juice (percentage to be at least 70 percent but not more than 95 percent)

Orange Juice Drink Containing ___ percent Orange Juice (percentage to be at least 35 percent but less than 70 percent)

Orange Drink Containing ___ percent Orange Juice (percentage to be at least 10 percent but less than 35 percent)

Orange Flavored Drink Containing ___ percent Orange Juice

(percentage to be less than 10 percent, but more than 0 percent)

Such standards are not in effect for other juices, but here is the common terminology:

Juice. The strained liquid (usually with a preservative added) from any fruit or vegetable (such as carrot juice or lemon juice), it is sold in cans, glass bottles, or jars. A great variety in sizes is offered, from individual serving units to institution sizes. Choose the approximate size for your needs. Remember that an open can on the refrigerator shelf will lose flavor and vitamin content after a few days, with the exception of bottled lemon juice.

Fruit juice drink. Usually consists of 50 percent fruit juice and 50 percent added water and sweeteners.

Fruit drink. Also a mixture of juice, water, and sweetener, but it does not require as large a percentage of juice. Orange drink, for example, may have less than 35 percent juice, but not less than 10 percent.

Nectar. The juice of a fruit such as the apricot that includes a major portion of the pulped fruit, or fruit purée. Therefore, it's a much thicker drink than a juice.

Concentrates. Juices that have been condensed down to four times their original strength. They are available in cans on the shelf or in the frozen food compartment. The usual ratio for reconstituting this product is to add three cans of water to one (same size) can of concentrate.

For information on comparative costs of frozen concentrate, canned, store-squeezed, and home-squeezed orange juice, see Chapter 6.

Soft Drinks, Bottled and Canned

Bottled and canned soft drinks, cola, orange, grape, root beer, ginger ale, and so on, are available in store brands, local brands, or national brands. Price and taste are the considerations here, as the nutritional value of carbonated beverages is almost entirely in their sugar content. Artificially sweetened soft drinks for those on low calorie diets have almost no nutritional value.

The question of throwaway cans and bottles versus returnable bottles for soft drinks and beer is an important issue. From the standpoint of your shopping plan, however, you might consider these guidelines: (1) If you and your family consume soft drinks on a fairly regular basis, you *should* probably buy them in large, returnable bottles; (2) If you consume soft drinks more moderately, you may want to buy cans or bottles on the basis of a prescribed allotment per family member per week or day; (3) If you use soft drinks only occasionally you may want to keep on hand a modest supply (parts of two 6-packs of cans or bottles of cola and ginger ale, for example) for guests. The 12-ounce cans or smaller bottles would probably be your best buy.

CHAPTER 10

Food Is What Nutrition Is All About

by Margaret L. Ross*

Nutrition is the science of food and its relation to health. It is concerned with the materials, or nutrients, in foods; what they do and why they are needed. The nutrients obtained from foods provide:

1. The energy or fuel (calories) required for body warmth and activities
2. The materials necessary for growth, maintenance, and repair of body tissues
3. The materials necessary for regulation of body processes

* Dr. Ross, now the director of nutrition for First National Stores Inc. in Somerville, Massachusetts, was formerly professor of nutrition and chairman of the department of home economics at Simmons College in Boston. She has also been a hospital dietitian and is coauthor of *Nutrition*, a widely used college textbook.

The nutrients required for these functions are divided into six classes: proteins, carbohydrates, fats, minerals, vitamins, and water.

Proteins

Proteins are essential constituents of every cell in the body and must be supplied in the diet for the building, maintenance, and repair of all tissues. Proteins are necessary also to:

1. Form hormones, such as insulin, thyroxin, and adrenalin, that regulate body processes
2. Form antibodies, such as gamma globulin, that fight infection
3. Make hemoglobin, the blood protein that carries oxygen to and carbon dioxide from the cells of the body
4. Supply energy

Proteins are combinations of somewhere between 18 and 22 small basic units called *amino acids*. All but eight of these can be manufactured in the body. These eight amino acids, therefore, must be supplied readymade in the food we eat. For this reason they are called the *essential* amino acids. Foods that contain all of the essential amino acids are referred to as *complete* in protein; those that lack or are limited in one or more of them are termed *incomplete*. Thus, the nutritive value of protein foods is assessed in terms of their amino acid makeup. Complete proteins generally come from foods of animal origin: meat, fish, poultry, eggs, milk, and milk products, such as cheese and ice cream. Proteins from plant sources, cereal grains, nuts, vegetables, and fruits, do not supply as good an assortment of amino acids as do those from animal sources. However, their contributions are important and, moreover, they are economical. Combinations of cereal and milk, rice and fish, spaghetti and meat or cheese, toast and an egg, and peanut butter, bread and milk all are excellent in meeting protein needs. The addition of a relatively small amount of a complete protein food to a somewhat larger amount of an incomplete protein food or a judicious combination of two incomplete protein foods enhances the protein value and makes the combinations complete in protein.

Carbohydrates

Carbohydrates are the most economical source of energy; when they are included in the diet in sufficient amounts less protein is used for energy purposes and more for tissue building and repair. They also help the body to use fats efficiently. Carbohydrates occur in foods chiefly in three forms: starches, sugars, and cellulose. Starches and sugars usually supply about half of the daily energy requirement. Cellulose, found in fruits, vegetables, and whole grain cereals, is not a nutrient; it supplies bulk or roughage which is needed for proper functioning of the intestines. Carbohydrates are found in cereals and products made from them such as bread and other baked goods; pastas, such as spaghetti, macaroni, and noodles; milk; fruits and vegetables; and sweets, such as sugar, syrups, jams and jellies, candy, soft drinks, and honey.

Fats

Fats are primarily a source of energy. They are also essential for the structure of the body since they make up a part of many cells. Weight for weight they supply a little more than twice as many calories (units of food energy) as carbohydrates or proteins. They are valuable because many of them provide significant amounts of fat-soluble vitamins and of the polyunsaturated fatty acids that are believed to be essential for good health. Fats also add flavor to foods, and they make meals satisfying because they digest and are absorbed slowly, thus delaying the onset of hunger.

Common sources of fat are butter, cream, ice cream, whole milk, most cheese, margarine, shortening, cooking and salad oils, mayonnaise, bacon and other fatty meats, egg yolk, nuts, chocolate, and foods such as pastries, candies, and snack items that are made with or are cooked in fat. The polyunsaturated fatty acids are supplied by liquid vegetable oils, corn, safflower, soybean, cottonseed, peanut, and by some fish oils and some nuts.

No discussion of fats would be complete without some mention of *cholesterol*. It is a fat-like substance made in the body and supplied in the diet in relatively smaller amounts by foods of animal origin. Cholesterol is a normal constituent of all body tissues, including the blood. In recent years the level of cholesterol in the blood has become a measure of the tendency to develop coronary heart disease. Although authorities do not all agree that diet is the primary factor in heart disease, they do suggest dietary modifications that have beneficial effects and reduce blood cholesterol levels. These include reducing the intake of total fat and cholesterol-containing foods, increasing the proportions of polyunsaturated fats and of starch-containing foods such as cereals and potatoes, and controlling calorie intake in order to maintain "normal" body weight.

When more carbohydrates, fats, and proteins are eaten than necessary, more calories are supplied than the daily energy expenditure requires. The extra calories are converted into body fat.

Minerals

Minerals are essential elements of bones and teeth, the hard structures of the body. They, also, are a necessary part of all cells and their presence in soft tissues and body fluids helps regulate many vital body processes. Altogether about 18 different minerals are needed. Those for which requirements have been established and about which most is known are *calcium, iron, iodine, magnesium,* and *phosphorus.*

Calcium. With phosphorus and vitamin D, it is necessary for the development and maintenance of strong bones and teeth. About 99 percent of the calcium in the body is in the bones and teeth. The other one percent, which is in body fluids and soft tissues, aids in proper heart, nerve, and muscle functioning and in blood clotting. The best sources of calcium are milk and milk products such as cheese and ice cream. Appreciable amounts are supplied by some dark-green leafy vegetables (broccoli, collards, kale, mustard greens, and turnip greens) and canned salmon if the bones are eaten. Other sources of calcium are dried peas and beans, crabmeat, clams, oysters, and enriched breads made with milk and milk solids.

Iron. Although it is needed by the body in much smaller amounts than calcium, it is a vital nutrient. It combines with protein with the help of copper to form *hemoglobin*, the red substance in blood that carries oxygen from the lungs to body cells and carbon dioxide from the cells to the lungs. Only a relatively few foods supply much iron. The main sources are lean meats, especially organ meats—liver, kidney, and heart—shellfish, dried peas and beans, dark-green leafy vegetables, dried fruits, egg yolks, and molasses. Enriched and whole grain cereal products are important sources if they are eaten frequently.

Iodine. This mineral is essential for the formation of *thyroxin*, a hormone produced in the thyroid gland that regulates many body functions including the rate at which energy is expended. Inadequate iodine intake causes *simple goiter*, which is an enlargement of the thyroid gland. Iodized salt, seafoods, and foods grown in iodine-rich soils near the seacoast are good sources of iodine. Meeting iodine requirements is usually not a problem for people who live close to the seacoast. However, those who live in inland areas where the soil is low in iodine may not get sufficient amounts of this mineral. The best way to be sure of an adequate intake of iodine, therefore, is to use iodized salt.

Magnesium and phosphorus. These are necessary for strong bones and teeth, and, like calcium, are found in largest amounts in these tissues. Both play important roles in the body's use of food for energy and in the proper utilization of other nutrients by body cells. Among other functions, magnesium is essential for the nervous control of muscles; phosphorus, for the absorption and transport of nutrients within the body. Magnesium is supplied by whole grain cereals, nuts, dried peas and beans, dark-green leafy vegetables, liver, potatoes, corn, dried fruits, and some seafoods. Phosphorus is found in a variety of foods. Meats, fish, eggs, milk and milk products, dried beans, and nuts are good sources. Diets that provide sufficient protein and calcium can be expected to supply enough phosphorus as well.

Vitamins

Vitamins are nutrients required in very small amounts for a variety of body processes. They are essential for the growth of body tissues, the release of energy from foods, and the proper functioning of nerves, muscles, and organs. A dozen or more major vitamins have been identified and each one tends to have specific vital functions. All of them will be provided in ample amounts by a good variety of fresh, frozen, and canned foods, so vitamin supplements should not be necessary for the normal healthy person. During pregnancy, infancy, and in certain disease conditions, however, vitamin needs are such that vitamin supplements are usually prescribed by physicians.

The vitamins are classified according to their solubility. Vitamins A, D, E and K are fat soluble; vitamin C and the B vitamins are water soluble.

Vitamin A. This nutrient is necessary for growth, normal night vision, and for keeping the skin, eyes, and inner linings of the body healthy and resistant to infection. Vitamin A is found only in foods of animal origin. Liver is an excellent source, and eggs, butter, margarine, whole milk, and cheese made from whole milk also supply significant amounts. Dark-green leafy vegetables and deep-yellow fruits and vegetables contribute to the vitamin A requirement because they contain a substance called *carotene* which is changed into vitamin A in the body. Broccoli, chard, spinach, kale, beet greens, carrots, winter squash, pumpkin, sweet potatoes, cantaloupe, apricots, and tomatoes all are rich in carotene and so are important sources of vitamin A.

Vitamin D. This vitamin makes the calcium and phosphorus supplied in foods available for body use. Further, it is essential for the formation and maintenance of strong bones and teeth. Few foods contain vitamin D naturally. Some is present in egg yolk, liver, and fish, especially sardines, salmon, herring, and tuna. Foods fortified with vitamin D such as fresh, evaporated, and dried nonfat milk supply most of the dietary vitamin. The major source of the vitamin is that produced by the action of direct sunlight on the skin. When the amount of sunshine is limited, supplements of this vitamin may be needed. However, a word of caution is necessary regarding both vitamin A and vitamin D. Overuse of supplements of these vitamins over a period of time produces toxic effects which are as serious as those of deficiencies of these vitamins.

Vitamin E. Known to be an essential nutrient for man, its exact functions in the body have not been determined. The best sources of vitamin E are salad oils, shortening, margarine, and green leafy vegetables. Meats, fish, poultry, and whole grains supply moderate amounts.

Vitamin K. An essential part of the blood-clotting mechanism, it is made in the body by microorganisms and also is found in a wide variety of foods. Since deficiencies of vitamins E and K are not found in the general population, it is assumed that adequate amounts of both of these vitamins are available in the food supply.

Vitamin C (Ascorbic Acid). Necessary for the formation and maintenance of the materials that hold body cells together and strengthen the walls of blood vessels. It also plays important roles in tooth and bone formation and in wound healing. Citrus fruits and raw green peppers are the richest sources of vitamin C. Strawberries, cantaloupe, pineapple, raw cabbage, broccoli, kale, collards, turnip and mustard greens are good sources. Potatoes and sweet potatoes are also good sources if they are cooked in the jacket.

The B Vitamins. Eleven vitamins or vitamin-like substances are in this group. The major ones that have been proven to be essential in human nutrition and for which requirements have been established are *thiamin (vitamin B_1), riboflavin (vitamin B_2), niacin, pyridoxine (vitamin B_6), folacin (folic acid)*, and *cobalamin (vitamin B_{12})*. *Biotin* and *pantothenic acid,* two other members of the B group, are essential nutrients, but their exact functions in the body and the amounts required in the diet have not been determined. The other three members of the group are *choline, inositol,* and *para-amino benzoic acid;* these may not be vitamins, but rather nutrient factors. All five of these are found in a wide variety of foods and are supplied in sufficient amounts when diets are adequate in other nutrients.

Thiamin, riboflavin, and *niacin* are required for the release of energy from foods, and for growth, good appetite and digestion, proper functioning of nerves, and healthy skin. In addition, riboflavin is essential for good vision. The leading sources of these vitamins are meats, especially organ meats, poultry, and fish. Whole grain and enriched cereal products, dried peas and beans, and vegetables all supply significant amounts of these vitamins.

Milk is an especially good source of riboflavin and pork, of thiamin. Niacin needs are met by the niacin supplied in foods, and also by a diet that includes a good amount of complete protein. This is because one of the essential amino acids, *tryptophan*, supplied in protein foods is converted into niacin in the body.

The other three major B-vitamins, *vitamin B₆, folic acid*, and *vitamin B₁₂*, are essential for the formation of red blood cells and therefore in the prevention of anemia. All three are necessary also for the utilization of proteins, carbohydrates, and fats; for growth; and for healthy nerve tissue. Vitamin B₆ and folic acid are supplied in a variety of foods of both plant and animal origin. Vitamin B₁₂ is found only in those of animal origin. Organ meats, liver and kidney, are excellent sources of all three of these vitamins. Additional significant amounts of vitamin B₆ are supplied by meats, poultry, fish, whole grain cereals, peanuts and peanut butter, potatoes, dried peas and beans, and most fruits and vegetables; additional amounts of folic acid by dark-green leafy vegetables, potatoes, and nuts; and of vitamin B₁₂ by milk.

Water

Water, although it is not always considered to be a nutrient, is essential for life; no human being can live more than a few days without it. Practically all body processes take place in solution, the essential substances or nutrients being dissolved in it. All body tissues contain water. Actually, two-thirds of body weight under normal conditions is water. Water lost in sweat, the breath, and through the intestinal tract and kidneys needs constant daily replacement. Sources are beverages, solid foods, most of which contain appreciable amounts of water, and that produced as a by-product when the body uses food for energy (metabolic water).

For good health, everyone must eat a well-chosen variety of foods that provide all the nutrients in required amounts and in proper relation to each other. In the daily food guide given in the appendix, foods are divided into four groups according to their similarity of nutrient content. Consult this guide for planning a well-balanced diet.

CHAPTER 11

Additives

A food additive is any substance that is added to food which may affect its characteristics by changing the taste, texture, appearance, nutritive qualities, or its "preservability." The use of additives has increased in recent years as research scientists have devised hundreds of new ways to improve or add *useful* characteristics to food. Note the word "useful" because the U.S. Food and Drug Administration, which controls the use of additives, requires that the manufacturer prove that the additive is safe for human consumption in normal use and that it has a useful purpose before approval is granted.

What Do Additives Do?

Without modern additives we would not have the quality and quantity of food now necessary to feed our nation's people. Specifically, additives may:

Enhance flavor. Examples are spices and natural and synthetic flavors.

Stabilize and thicken. Starch, pectin, gelatin, gum arabic, agar and *methyl cellulose* are among those used.

Neutralize or alter acidity or alkalinity. Quality production of many types of baked goods, soft drinks, and confectionery requires this.

Prevent oxidation and spoilage. People have long used salt, sugar, vinegar, heat, freezing, smoke, and spices to prevent or delay food spoilage. Modern science has developed preservatives such as *sodium* and *calcium propionate* (produced naturally in Swiss cheese) to retard the growth of bread molds, and *BHT (butylated hydroxytoluene)* and *BHA (butylated hydroxyanisole)* to retard the oxidation that allows fats and fatty foods to become rancid.

Other additives retain moisture, add nutrients such as vitamins and minerals, mature and bleach flour, increase volume and smoothness, and act as propellants for food in pressurized cans. Additives are also used for hardening, drying, coloring, leavening, non-caloric sweetening, disease prevention, creaming, firming, whipping, sterilizing, and against foaming and sticking.

The amounts of additives vary with the type of food, the additive's safety, and the least amount needed to accomplish the desired result. For example, in dry cereal the amount of BHT or BHA allowed is 50 parts per million. The Food and Drug Administration scientists estimate that if BHT and BHA were used at the maximum level in all foods in which it is authorized, the maximum daily intake would be about 4 parts per million. The actual usage is substantially less. But 4 parts per million equals only 128/1000 of 1 ounce of each ton of food, or 4 parts per million of all the food a person might eat in a normal lifetime; this amount would equal about four mouthfuls.

Of course, any additive can be harmful in certain amounts or under certain circumstances. Such common additives as sugar and salt, for example, which are quite safe in ordinary amounts for healthy people can pose problems for the diabetic or heart patient if not used in controlled amounts.

The fact that additives are chemicals should not be a cause of concern. We casually use in our kitchen, salt, baking powder, vinegar, soda, cornstarch, cream of tartar, and water without thinking that we are using sodium chloride, calcium acid phosphate, acetic acid, sodium acid carbonate, amylum, potassium bitartrate, and hydrogen oxide.

"Natural" or Health Foods

Closely allied to the concern about the adding of chemicals to foods is the controversy about possible danger in the use of chemicals, primarily pesticides and fertilizers, in the growing of foodstuffs. Production of food without chemicals is known as *organic farming*. Many stores have a special section of "health" foods or of so-called natural foods. Here they stock foods for special health purposes, for example, diabetic and low-sodium diets, or foods which have fewer or no chemical additives or have been subjected to little or no processing, whole wheat flour or whole grain *granola* cereals. Some of the natural foods will be found in the regular section of the store. Unbleached white flour, for instance, may be right next to the artificially matured or *bleached* flour. The unbleached flour may or may not be enriched. (See the section on enrichment in Chapter 5.)

As a shopper, the major point you need to remember is that foods promoted for their natural or unprocessed qualities are likely to be higher priced than the regular products.

The accompanying chart of commonly used additives prepared in consultation with the Food and Drug Administration can help you to identify some of the unfamiliar names on the labels of food.

FOOD ADDITIVES

Type and Purpose of Food Additive	Names of Some Commonly Used Additives	Partial Listing of Foods Containing Additives
Preservatives		
Inhibit or prevent growth of microbes and retard spoilage	Sodium propionate Calcium propionate Sodium sorbate Potassium sorbate Citric acid[a] Lactic acid[a] Benzoic acid BHA (Butylated hydroxyanisole) BHT (Butylated hydroxytoluene) Sodium benzoate Sorbic acid Sulphur dioxide	Baked goods Processed cheeses Syrup Jams Pie fillings Margarine Mayonnaise Salad and cooking oils Shortening Sauces Fruit juices Fruit drinks Fruit cocktails Carbonated beverages Beer
Antioxidants		
Prevent or retard rancidity in foods that usually contain fats and oils	Propyl gallate BHA BHT Ascorbic acid (Vitamin C)[b] Citric acid[b] Phosphoric acid Erythorbic acid Sodium erythorbate Sodium sulfite Potassium sulfite Sodium bisulfite	Canned fruits Canned vegetables Breakfast cereals Cakes and cake mixes Ice cream Butter Salad and cooking oils Shortenings Processed meats Jams and jellies Soft drinks
Sequestrants		
Bind and inactivate trace metals such as copper	Calcium (Disodium ethylene diamine) EDTA Citric acid Sodium citrate Tetrasodium pyrophosphate Disodium phosphate	Cheese Ice cream Bread Breakfast cereals Cake and cake mixes Margarine Mayonnaise Salad and cooking oils Jams and jellies Pie fillings Vinegars Soft drinks

[a] When acidity is sufficiently changed.
[b] When used with BHA or BTA.

Type and Purpose of Food Additive	Names of Some Commonly Used Additives	Partial Listing of Foods Containing Additives
Emulsifiers and Surfactants Permit the dispersion of one liquid into another and prevent separation of liquids	Lecithin Mono and diglycerides Monosodium phosphate Sodium phosphate Glyceryl lacto stearate Polysorbate 60 Polysorbate 80 Propylene glycol monostearate Glyceryl lacto stearate Sodium stearoyl-2-lactylate Sorbitan monostearate	Ice cream Bread Cakes and cake mixes Margarine Salad and cooking oils Peanut butter Gelatin desserts Desserts Soft drinks Beer
Stabilizers and Thickeners Improve the consistency of a food and permit the suspension of solids in liquids	Carrageenan Sodium alginate Gum acacia Gum tragacanth Cellulose gum Guar gum Sodium carboxymethylcellulose Dextrin Gelatin Starches	Chocolate products Chocolate milk Ice cream, sherbets, and frozen custards Syrup for frozen products Pressure-dispersed whipped cream Condiments Salad dressings Baked goods and icings Gelatin desserts Dessert mixes Cake mixes Cream cheese Cheese spreads Meat products Beer
Coloring agents Add or restore color of food that may be lost in processing	Cochineal Tumeric Annatto Synthetic water soluble dyes	Cereals Crackers and cookies Cakes and cake mixes Cheese Ice cream Butter Margarine Salad and cooking oils Fruits and vegetables Jams and jellies Soft drinks

Type and Purpose of Food Additive	Names of Some Commonly Used Additives	Partial Listing of Foods Containing Additives
Leavening agents		
Gas formers causing dough to rise	Yeast Baking powder (sodium bicarbonate, calcium mono or dibasic phosphate and starch) Baking soda Sodium bicarbonate glucono delta lactone Sodium aluminum phosphate Sodium acid pyro phosphate	Cakes Cake mixes Bread and other baking products
Buffers, acids, and alkalis		
Make foods more or less acid	Citric acid Acetic acid Fumaric acid Adipic acid Phosphoric acid Malic acid Sodium citrate Tartaric acid Lactic acid Calcium phosphate Monosodium phosphate Potassium citrate	Processed cheese Ices and sherbets Cream pies Desserts Pie fillings Pastry products Candies Jams and jellies Soups Olives Canned vegetables Fruit flavored gelatin Fruit drinks Carbonated beverages Wines
Bleaching and Maturing agents		
Used in milling flour to remove natural yellow color and to improve texture of dough	Acetone peroxides Azodicarbonamide Benzoyl peroxide Chlorine Hydrogen peroxide	Bread flour Cake flour Cheese Cheese whey

Type and Purpose of Food Additive	Names of Some Commonly Used Additives	Partial Listing of Foods Containing Additives
Firming and Anti-caking agents Prevent softening of fruits and vegetables and also prevent caking of products by preventing absorption of moisture	Calcium stearate Calcium chloride Calcium citrate Calcium phosphate Calcium gluconate Sodium silico aluminate Sodium aluminum sulfate Corn starch Potassium iodide Cuprous iodide Potassium ferrocyanide	Canned fruits Canned vegetables Salt and other seasonings Sugar Dried powders
Flavoring agents Improve, enhance, mask, or change the flavor of foods	Essential oils, natural and synthetic Amyl acetate (banana) Allyl caproate (pineapple) Anathole (licorice) Carvone (mint) Cinnamaldehyde (cinnamon) Ethyl pelargonate (brandy) Natural herbs and spices (pepper, oregano, etc.)	Most canned and packaged foods
Nutrient supplements Improve or restore the nutrient composition of a product	Thiamin Niacin Riboflavin Iron Ascorbic acid (Vitamin C) Vitamin A Vitamin D Calcium salts Iodine	Breads Cereals Products made with enriched flour Fruit juices Fruit drinks Margarine Milk Instant meals Salt Snack foods

CHAPTER 12

Who Protects Our Food?

The title of this chapter seems a simple question; most people would say the government. They'd be right, but only partially so.

In reality, food protection is a partnership among many federal government agencies with responsibility for food protection, state and local agencies with inspection or enforcement functions, research laboratories and scientists in colleges and universities and in the food industry, and you, the consumer. You're the final link in the food protection chain because how you handle and store food once you've bought it can make the vital difference between whether it's good and safe to eat or not. Detailed charts on food storage are included in the appendix.

In addition, you and your spokesmen play important roles in keeping government food protection laws and procedures adequate and enforced. Whether the consumer's voice is heard through the office of the President's Special Assistant for Consumer Affairs* or through one of the many private organizations which represent consumers, it's being listened to in Congress, in government, and in the food industry.

Another important force in food protection is the food industry. Legitimate food manufacturers and food retailers have money-back policies which enable the customers to return food that is found unsatisfactory for any reason. Therefore, it is in their interest to sell good quality products.

To help you learn what the government agencies concerned with food protection actually do, here's a brief description of them and the programs they administer.

Food and Drug Administration (FDA)

The agency most directly involved in consumer protection in all areas is the Food and Drug Administration (FDA), a part of the U.S. Department of Health, Education and Welfare.

FDA administers the nation's basic food and drug law, the Federal Food, Drug, and Cosmetic Act, as well as the Federal Hazardous Substances Act and several others. FDA's official mission is to insure that foods are safe, pure, and wholesome; drugs and therapeutic devices are safe and effective; cosmetics are harmless; and that all these products are honestly and informatively labeled and packaged.

To accomplish this, FDA employs some 4,700 men and women, scientists, physicians, inspectors, technicians, and many others. In the food area, FDA inspectors periodically check processing and storage plants to insure that they are sanitary. They also check the wholesomeness of ingredients and finished food products and the legality of the packages and labels.

FDA is active in the prevention of food-borne disease. Because so much of the nation's food originates in the comparatively few

* Mrs. Virginia Knauer currently heads this office.

"kitchens" of the major manufacturers, disease carried by a single contaminated product can affect many people. Whenever contamination by bacteria, such as salmonella, is discovered, FDA works to locate and eliminate the source, in addition to removing the contaminated food from store shelves.

The agency carries on cooperative programs with state and local health authorities to insure safe milk supplies and to see that shellfish are harvested from unpolluted waters. It also sees that chemical additives in foods—preservatives, artificial flavors, and colors— are safe, and it sets standards for some foods, making sure that, for example, your catsup has a certain minimum amount of tomato in it.

Standards of identity have been set up for more than 200 basic food items and they prevent watering down of products by defining what a food should contain—what you are entitled to receive when you purchase the food by its common or usual name. For example, fruit jams must contain 45 parts of fruit and 55 parts of sugar or other sweetener, and raisin bread must have raisins equaling 50 percent of the weight of the flour.

Manufacturers who wish to enrich certain foods must follow the requirements in FDA's standards for *enriched, fortified* or *restored* foods. Flour, bread, degerminated corn meal, corn grits, whole grain corn meal, and white rice may be enriched with thiamin, riboflavin, niacin, and iron. These same B vitamins and iron may be retained or restored in food cereals. FDA controls the levels of enrichment, just as it controls the amount of other vitamins or minerals which may be added to foods. If milk is to be fortified with vitamin D and advertised as such, FDA stipulates that the fortification must be sufficient to have a meaningful nutritional impact. The same stipulation applies to vitamin A, which is added to milk and margarine, and to vitamin C, which is added to juices, ades, and drinks in prescribed amounts. (For additional comments on enrichment and fortification see Chapter 5.)

For canned fruits and vegetables, the FDA standards of quality set minimum specifications for such factors as tenderness, color, and freedom from defects. Quality standards for canned foods, for example, limit the "string" in green beans, excessive peel in tomatoes, hardness in peas, "soupiness" in cream-style corn, and pits in pitted canned cherries.

In its specialized research laboratories in Washington and around the country, FDA tests products picked up by inspectors from factories, warehouses, and stores in a continuous watch over the food supply.

It pays particular attention to foods for special dietary uses, such as foods for low-salt and diabetic diets, low calorie foods, and infant foods. FDA assures that the special properties claimed for these foods are indeed possessed by them and that misleading health claims are not made.

Finally, FDA makes sure that your foods are honestly and informatively labeled. Ingredients must be listed (except for standardized foods on which only optional ingredients need be given), and the net weight must be prominently displayed so that the consumer can compare values.

The agency encourages consumers to report cases of foods or other items that are mislabeled, unsanitary, or otherwise harmful. You simply call or write the nearest of FDA's 17 district offices. (See the accompanying list of addresses and telephone numbers.)

FOOD AND DRUG ADMINISTRATION DISTRICT OFFICES

Office	Address	Area Code and Number
Atlanta	60 Eighth Street, N.E. Altanta, Georgia 30309	404 526–5265
Baltimore	900 Madison Avenue Baltimore, Maryland 21201	301 962–3396
Boston	585 Commercial Street Boston, Massachusetts 02109	617 223–3174
Buffalo	599 Delaware Avenue Buffalo, New York 14202	716 842–6906
Chicago	Main Post Office Building 433 W. Van Buren Street, Room 1222 Chicago, Illinois 60607	312 353–5863
Cincinnati	Paul B. Dunbar Building 1141 Central Parkway Cincinnati, Ohio 45202	513 684–3503
Dallas	3032 Bryan Street Dallas, Texas 75204	214 749–2735
Denver	513 U. S. Customhouse Denver, Colorado 80202	303 837–4335

FOOD AND DRUG ADMINISTRATION DISTRICT OFFICES (continued)

Office	Address	Area Code and Number	
Detroit	1560 E. Jefferson Avenue Detroit, Michigan 48207	313	226–6260
Kansas City	1009 Cherry Street Kansas City, Missouri 64106	816	374–5521
Los Angeles	Walter G. Campbell Building 1521 W. Pico Boulevard Los Angeles, California 90015	216	688–3771
Minneapolis	240 Hennepin Avenue Minneapolis, Minnesota 55401	612	725–2121
New Orleans	U. S. Customhouse Building 423 Canal Street, Room 222 New Orleans, Louisiana 70130	504	527–2401
New York	850 Third Avenue, Room 700 Brooklyn, New York 11232	212	788–1300
Philadelphia	Room 1204, U. S. Customhouse Second & Chestnut Streets Philadelphia, Pennsylvania 19106	215	597–4390
San Francisco	Federal Office Building 50 Fulton Street, Room 526 San Francisco, California 94102	415	566–2062
Seattle	Federal Office Building 901 First Avenue, Room 5003 Seattle, Washington 98104	206	442–5304

A recent FDA fact sheet gives the following guidelines on how to report:

1. Report your grievance promptly, giving your name, address, telephone number and directions to residence or place of business.
2. State clearly what appears to be wrong.
3. Describe the label of the product and give any code marks that appear on the container. (In the case of a canned food, these are usually embossed into or stamped on the lid of the can.)
4. Give the name and address of the store where the item was bought and the date of purchase.

5. Save whatever remains of the suspect product or the empty container for your doctor's guidance or possible examination by FDA.
6. Hold any unopened container of the product bought at the same time.
7. If any injury is involved, see a doctor at once.
8. Also report the suspect product to the manufacturer, packer, or distributor shown on the label of the product and to the store where you bought it.

Of course, the number and kinds of protection FDA provides you are constantly changing. New regulations and laws are always being proposed in an effort to provide greater protection. At the moment, new ingredient and nutrient labeling requirements are under consideration; in cooperation with FDA, several supermarket chains are voluntarily testing nutrient labeling plans—letting you know the nutritional value of the foods you buy.

United States Department of Agriculture (USDA)

The other Federal agency that is deeply involved in protecting food is the U.S. Department of Agriculture (USDA), primarily through its Consumer and Marketing Service. USDA's major programs revolve around the inspection and grading of meat and poultry products. Explanations have already been given in Chapter 2 on how to use these USDA standards as guides for selection of meat, poultry, and eggs. But since, on the average, you spend a third of your family food budget for these foods, an understanding of how these standards are administered can also be useful.

The USDA Inspection Program

The inspection program is required by law and is responsible for wholesomeness and proper labeling. To pass inspection, meat and poultry products must be from healthy animals and birds which were handled or processed under strict sanitary conditions, must not be adulterated, and must be truthfully packaged and labeled. The circular mark of federal meat inspection appears as a purple stamp on retail meat cuts (see below, left). Because only the major cuts of the carcass are marked, this stamp may not appear on every roast or steak you buy. In addition, all fresh or processed meat products (from sausages to spreads) that are shipped from one state to another must have the mark of federal inspection (see below, center).

The chilled or frozen ready-to-cook poultry offered in the supermarket as well as the canned, frozen, dehydrated and other forms of poultry products also must carry the USDA inspection mark (see below, right).

Left and center: USDA meat inspection marks; right: poultry inspection marks.

The inspection process is comprehensive and thorough and covers all plants selling across state lines or to other countries. To be sure that food is pure throughout the process, inspection occurs at various stages. USDA must approve the layout of each federally inspected plant, as well as the equipment and facilities, to assure that they lend themselves to proper cleaning and to sanitary operation. An inspector examines the equipment in a plant to make sure that it is clean before work begins each day and continues checking operations in the slaughtering or processing plant to ascertain that products are handled properly and that equipment is kept clean. The checking process continues through the packaging and labeling process, and finally spot checking may be done in the warehouse or store.

USDA also reviews foreign inspection systems and packing plants which export meat and poultry to this country and then reinspect imported products at the various ports of entry to the United States.

USDA Grading Program

The other program administered by USDA's Consumer and Marketing Service is grading for quality. Although grading is a voluntary service to meat packers, poultry and egg processors, and others who request it and pay for the service, more than half the beef and three-fourths of the poultry on the market is graded. Federal inspection is required if the food is to be graded.

The federally graded meats carry a purple grade, a shield enclosing the letters *USDA* and the grade name. Grade stamps appear on most retail cuts of beef, veal, calf, lamb, and mutton, but pork is not usually graded. *USDA Prime,* the top grade, is used largely by hotels and restaurants. *USDA Choice* and *USDA Good* are the grades most commonly found in retail markets (see below). Some meat packers, wholesalers, and retailers, however, use their own brand names to designate the quality levels of their products.

USDA meat grade marks

Poultry must be USDA-inspected before it can be federally graded. The grades for poultry are based on meatiness, freedom

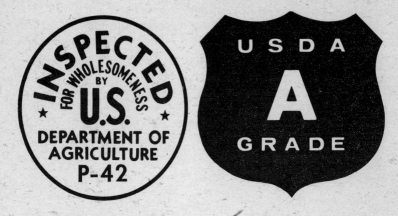

USDA inspection and grade marks for poultry. *Left:* assurance of whole-someness; *right:* assurance of quality.

from defects, and general appearance. The top grade of poultry is marked *USDA Grade A.* This is the only grade you are likely to find in your supermarket. Poultry of Grades B and C is more generally used in processed foods. The poultry grade label also suggests suitable cooking methods and indicates the age of the poultry.

USDA grade and size shield for eggs

For example, the grade shield for chicken might be: *Broiler or fryer, young hen, young tom,* or *mature turkey*.

Eggs are nearly always found with grade indication, because many states have laws requiring that eggs be graded before they are sold retail. Federally graded eggs are identified with the shield-shaped grade mark which indicates the quality at the time of grading. Quality is based on specific conditions of shell, air cell, yolk, and white. The quality grades rank from *U.S. Grade AA* (or *Fresh Fancy*), *Grade A,* to *Grade B*. In addition, eggs are classified by size according to weight per dozen. Common market sizes of eggs and the minimum weight per dozen range as follows: *U.S. Extra Large*: 27 ounces; *U.S. Large*: 24 ounces; *U.S. Medium*: 21 ounces; and *U.S. Small*: 18 ounces.

The size is independent of quality—large eggs may be of high or low quality and high quality eggs may be of any size. Therefore, in buying eggs the consumer must consider both grade and weight in relation to the price of eggs and must evaluate this also in relation to the purpose.

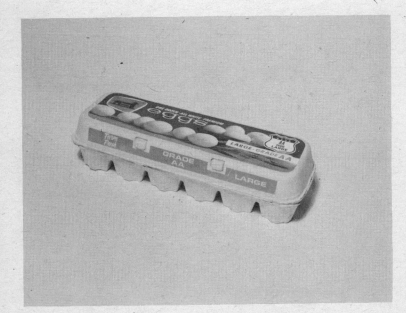

Find it on the carton or on a tape sealing the carton.

USDA grade shield for butter

Grade AA or Grade A eggs are excellent for all purposes, but are especially good for poaching and frying, in which the appearance of the finished product is important. Grade B eggs are satisfactory for use in cooked dishes. The substitution of one egg size for another often makes little difference in recipe results.

Butter also is covered by the USDA grading system. The *U.S. Grade AA* and *Grade A* are the quality ratings most often seen and are given to butter made from fresh, sweet cream that rates high on its texture, spreadability, and flavor. There is also a

USDA U.S. Extra grade shield for instant nonfat dry milk

Grade B butter, which is generally made from selected sour cream. As with meat and poultry grading, the manufacturing plant must meet exacting requirements on the basis of official written standards to earn the right to use USDA grade shields for butter. Also, tests are run on the butter's "keeping quality" as a check for wholesomeness.

Nonfat dry milk is another dairy product that may be graded. When you see the *U.S. Extra* grade shield on nonfat dry milk packages, it means that the product meets the standards for sweet, pleasing flavor, natural color, and it will dissolve instantly when mixed with water.

Fruits and vegetables also have grade standards established by the USDA. The standards are used by processors, buyers, and others in wholesale trading as a help in ascertaining value. If a fruit or vegetable is packed under continuous USDA inspection, the individual cans and packages may carry the U.S. grade name.

The top grade in most cases for fruit in a package is *U.S. Fancy* or *U.S. No. 1*. The vegetable grades are *U.S. Grade A* or *Fancy; U.S. Grade B* or *Extra Standard;* and *U.S. Grade C* or *Standard.* Whenever the U.S. shields bearing the grade names or the state-

USDA grade shield for fresh fruits and vegetables

ment "Packed under continuous inspection of the U.S. Department of Agriculture" appears on canned or frozen fruits or vegetables, this is a signal of designated quality to the buyer. However, most canned and frozen vegetables are packed and priced according to their quality, even though a grade is not shown on a label. Sometimes the grade name is indicated without the *U.S.* in front of it, as, for example, *Grade A* or *Fancy*, but the product must measure up to the quality stated, even though it has not been officially inspected for grade.

USDA grade shield for canned, frozen, and dried fruits and vegetables. It is also used on a few related products like honey, jam, and jelly.

The USDA is concerned with many other programs of research and inspection. Frequently these are carried on in conjunction with state departments of agriculture and the state experiment station research activities in the state university systems. In many cases these state agencies are in a better position to provide help in problems that are peculiar to their states.

Other Agencies

Of course there are many other federal and state agencies that are concerned with food protection. Fish is the responsibility of the U.S. Department of Interior's Bureau of Fisheries, and there is an established inspection and grading service for fish that uses shield marks similar to the meat grading system to identify high quality seafoods. The U.S. Public Health Service, which like the FDA is a part of the Department of Health, Education, and Welfare, assists states and municipalities in the preparation of laws for the prevention and control of diseases—particularly those which can be transmitted through shellfish, milk, and foods served to the public through restaurants and through vending machines. The Milk Ordinance and Code recommended by the Public Health Service has been adopted by many states.

Still other aspects of protection related to food resources come under the Federal Trade Commission, which concerns itself with unfair trade practices and with false or misleading advertising. The Atomic Eenergy Commission is responsible for the control of radiation in food and food products.

In addition, many private agencies and industry trade associations set and enforce standards for products that are sometimes higher than those required by the government.

Appendix

COST OF FOOD AT HOME

U.S. Average Estimated for Food Plans at Three Cost Levels,
March 1972[a]

Sex-age groups[b]	Cost for 1 week			Cost for 1 month		
	Low-cost plan	Moderate-cost plan	Liberal plan	Low-cost plan	Moderate-cost plan	Liberal plan
Families	Dollars	Dollars	Dollars	Dollars	Dollars	Dollars
Family of 2:						
20 to 35 years[c]	19.40	24.60	30.50	83.70	107.00	131.80
55 to 75 years[c]	15.80	20.60	24.80	68.50	89.30	107.70
Family of 4:						
Preschool children[d]	28.10	35.70	43.70	121.40	155.20	189.30
School children[e]	32.60	41.70	51.40	140.90	180.90	222.80
Individuals[f]						
Children under						
1 year	3.70	4.70	5.30	16.10	20.40	22.80
1 to 3 years	4.80	6.00	7.20	20.70	26.10	31.30
3 to 6 years	5.70	7.30	8.80	24.60	31.80	38.20
6 to 9 years	6.90	8.90	11.10	29.90	38.50	48.30
Girls						
9 to 12 years	7.90	10.20	12.00	34.10	44.20	52.00
12 to 15 years	8.70	11.30	13.70	37.50	49.00	59.60
15 to 20 years	8.90	11.20	13.40	38.40	48.70	58.10
Boys						
9 to 12 years	8.10	10.40	12.60	34.90	45.10	54.70
12 to 15 years	9.40	12.50	14.90	40.80	54.00	64.50
15 to 20 years	10.90	13.90	16.80	47.20	60.10	72.80

[a] Estimates computed from quantities in food plans published in *Family Economics Review,* October 1964. Costs of the plans were first estimated by using average price per pound of each food group paid by urban survey families at 3 income levels in 1965. These prices were adjusted to current levels by use of *Retail Food Prices by Cities,* released by the Bureau of Labor Statistics.

[b] Persons of the first age listed up to but not including the second age.

[c] 10 percent added for family size adjustment.

[d] Man and woman, 20 to 35 years; children 1 to 3 and 3 to 6 years.

[e] Man and woman, 20 to 35 years; child 6 to 9; and boy 9 to 12 years.

[f] Costs given for persons in families of 4. For other size families, adjust thus: 1-person, add 20 percent; 2-person, add 10 percent; 3-person, add 5 percent; 5-person, subtract 5 percent; 6-or-more-person, subtract 10 percent.

COST OF FOOD AT HOME (continued)

Sex-age groups[b]	Cost for 1 week			Cost for 1 month		
	Low-cost plan	Moderate-cost plan	Liberal plan	Low-cost plan	Moderate-cost plan	Liberal plan
Individuals (continued)						
Women						
20 to 35 years	8.20	10.40	12.60	35.30	45.20	54.60
35 to 55 years	7.80	10.00	12.10	33.90	43.50	52.60
55 to 75 years	6.60	8.60	10.30	28.70	37.40	44.80
75 years and over	6.00	7.70	9.40	26.00	33.20	40.80
Pregnant	9.70	12.20	14.40	42.00	52.70	62.50
Nursing	11.20	14.00	16.40	48.70	60.60	71.10
Men						
20 to 35 years	9.40	12.00	15.10	40.80	52.10	65.20
35 to 55 years	8.70	11.20	13.70	37.90	48.40	59.40
55 to 75 years	7.80	10.10	12.20	33.60	43.80	53.10
75 years and over	7.20	9.70	11.80	31.40	42.20	51.10

SOURCE: *Family Economics Review*. Washington, D.C.: U.S. Department of Agriculture, March 1972, p. 25.

YIELDS AND EQUIVALENTS OF SOME COMMON FOODS

Product	Weight	Measure or Number	Yield
Almond (kernels)	¼ pound		¾ cup kernels
Almonds (in shell)	1 pound		1½ cups kernels
Bread (dry)		1 (⅝" slice)	⅓ cup dry bread crumbs
Bread (fresh)		1 (⅝" slice)	1 cup soft cubes or crumbs
Bread (loaf)	1 pound		20 slices (varies 12–26 slices)
Butter or margarine	¼ pound	1 stick	½ cup
Cereal flakes		3 cups (approx.)	1⅓ cups fine crumbs
Cheese (cheddar)	¼ pound		1 cup grated
Coffee (ground)	1 pound	5 cups	40 to 50 cups
Coffee (instant)	2 ounces	1 cup	25 to 30 cups
Cornmeal, yellow	1 pound		3 cups
Cottage cheese	½ pound	½ pint	1 cup
Crackers (graham)		15	1 cup fine crumbs
Crackers (soda)		22	1 cup fine crumbs
Flour (all-purpose)	1 pound		4 cups sifted

YIELDS AND EQUIVALENTS OF SOME COMMON FOODS (continued)

Product	Weight	Measure or Number	Yield
Flour (cake)	1 pound		4¾ cups sifted
Kidney beans	1 pound	2½ cups	6¾ cups cooked
Lemon (fresh)		1	3 to 4 tablespoons juice
Lima beans (large), dried		1 cup	2½ cups cooked (approx.)
Lima beans (small), dried		1 cup	2 cups cooked (approx.)
Macaroni, 1"	1 pound	4 cups	9 cups cooked
Marshmallows	¼ pound		16 regular size
Navy beans	1 pound	2⅓ cups	6 cups cooked
Nonfat dry milk (crystals)	1 pound	5⅔ cups	4¼ quarts milk
Nonfat dry milk (powder)	1 pound	4 cups	5 quarts milk
Noodles	1 pound	6 to 8 cups	9 cups cooked
Onion		1 medium	⅔ to 1 cup chopped
Orange (fresh)		1	6 to 8 tablespoons juice
Peanut butter	1 pound		2 cups
Pecans (kernels)	¼ pound		1 cup halves, ⅞ cup chopped
Pecans (in shell)	1 pound		2¼ cups halves, 2 cups chopped
Raisins, seedless	½ pound		1½ cups whole, 1 cup chopped
Spaghetti	1 pound	4¾ cups	10 cups cooked
Split peas	1 pound	2 cups	5¼ cups cooked
Sugar (brown)	1 pound		2¼ cups firmly packed
Sugar (confectioner's)	1 pound		3½ cups sifted
Sugar (granulated)	1 pound		2¼ cups
Sugar (granulated superfine)	1 pound		2⅓ cups
Tea	1 pound	6 to 8 cups	300 cups
Walnut (kernels)	¼ pound		1 cup halves
	³⁄₁₀ pound		1 cup chopped
Walnuts (in shell)	1 pound		1½ to 2 cups kernels
Whipping cream		½ pint (1 cup)	2 cups whipped

SOURCE: *Food Yields and Measures.* University of California Agricultural Extension Service, Pub. HXT–20.

CUPBOARD STORAGE CHART

Temperature: Store foods in your coolest cabinets—away from appliances which produce heat.

Time: Many staples and canned foods have a relatively long shelf life, but buy only what you expect to use within the time recommended in the chart for each product. Date food packages and use the oldest first. Geographic area will affect recommended storage time. Warm and humid climates shorten the shelf life of foods.

Purchasing: Buy fresh-looking packages. Dusty cans or torn labels may indicate old stock. Carefully check dented cans before buying. Do not purchase bulging cans.

Food	Recommended storage time at 70° F.	Handling hints
Staples		
Baking powder	18 months or expiration date on can	Keep dry and covered.
Baking soda	2 years	Keep dry and covered.
Bouillon cubes or granules	2 years	Keep dry and covered.
Bread crumbs, dried	6 months	Keep dry and covered.
Cereals		
ready-to-eat (unopened)	6–12 months*	
ready-to-eat (opened)	2–3 months	Refold package liner tightly after opening.
cooked	6 months	
Chocolate, premelted	12 months	Keep cool.
semi-sweet	2 years	Keep cool.
unsweetened	18 months	Keep cool.
Chocolate syrup		
(unopened)	2 years*	
(opened)	6 months	Cover tightly. Refrigerate after opening.
Cocoa mixes	8 months	Cover tightly.
Coffee		
cans (unopened)	2 years*	
cans (opened)	2 weeks	Refrigerate after opening;
instant (unopened)	1–2 years*	keep tightly closed. Use dry
instant (opened)	2 weeks	measuring spoon.
Coffee lighteners (dry)		
(unopened)	9 months*	
(opened)	6 months	Keep lid tightly closed.

CUPBOARD STORAGE CHART (continued)

Food	Recommended storage time at 70° F.	Handling hints
Staples (continued)		
Cornmeal	12 months	Keep tightly closed.
Cornstarch	18 months	Keep tightly closed.
Flour, white	6–8 months	Keep in airtight container.
whole wheat	6–8 months	Keep refrigerated. Store in airtight container.
Gelatin, all types	18 months	Keep in original container.
Grits	12 months	Store in airtight container.
Honey	12 months	Cover tightly. If crystallizes, warm jar in pan of hot water.
Jellies, jams	12 months	Cover tightly. Storage life lengthened if refrigerated after opening. White mold spots can be removed and product used.
Molasses (unopened)	12 months+*	
(opened)	6 months	Keep tightly closed. Refrigerate to extend storage life. Remove any light surface mold, and use.
Marshmallow cream (unopened)	3–4 months	Cover tightly. Refrigerate after opening to extend storage life. Serve at room temperature.
Marshmallows	2–3 months	Keep in airtight container.
Mayonnaise (unopened)	2–3 months	Refrigerate after opening.
Milk		
condensed or evaporated (unopened)	12 months	Invert cans every 2 months.
nonfat dry (unopened)	6 months*	
(opened)	3 months	Put in airtight container.
Pasta (spaghetti, macaroni, etc.)	2 years	Once opened, store in airtight container.
Pectin, liquid (opened)	1 month	Recap and refrigerate.
Rice, white	2 years+	Keep tightly closed.
flavored or herb	6 months	
Salad dressings		
bottled (unopened)	10–12 months*	

CUPBOARD STORAGE CHART (continued)

Food	Recommended storage time at 70° F.	Handling hints
Staples (continued)		
Salad dressings		
bottled (opened)	3 months	Refrigerate after opening.
made from mix	2 weeks	Refrigerate prepared dressing.
Salad oils (unopened)	6 months*	
(opened)	1–3 months	Refrigerate after opening.
Shortenings, solid	8 months	Refrigeration not needed.
Sugar		
brown	4 months	Put in airtight container.
confectioner's	18 months	Put in airtight container.
granulated	2 years+	Cover tightly.
artificial sweeteners	2 years+	Cover tightly.
Syrups	12 months	Keep tightly closed. Refrigerate to extend storage life. Remove any light surface mold, and use.
Tea		
bags	18 months	Put in airtight container.
instant	3 years	Cover tightly.
loose	2 years	Put in airtight container.
Vinegar		
(unopened)	2 years+*	
(opened)	12 months	Keep tightly closed. Slightly cloudy appearance doesn't affect quality. Distilled vinegar keeps longer than cider vinegar.
Mixes and packaged foods		
Biscuit, brownie, muffin mix	9 months	Keep cool and dry.
Cakes, purchased	1–2 days	If butter-cream, whipped cream or custard frostings, fillings, refrigerate.
Cake mixes	9 months	Keep cool and dry.
angel food	12 months	
Casseroles, complete or add own meat	9–12 months	Keep cool and dry.
Cookies, homemade	2–3 weeks	Put in airtight container.
packaged	2 months	Keep box tightly closed.

CUPBOARD STORAGE CHART (continued)

Food	Recommended storage time at 70° F.	Handling hints
Mixes and packaged foods (continued)		
Crackers	8 months	Keep box tightly closed.
Frosting, canned	3 months	Store leftovers in refrigerator.
mix	8 months	
Hot-roll mix	18 months	If opened, put in airtight container.
Pancake mix	6–9 months	Put in airtight container.
Piecrust mix	8 months	Keep cool and dry.
Pies and pastries	2–3 days	Refrigerate whipped cream, custard and chiffon fillings.
Potatoes, instant	6–12 months	Keep in airtight package.
Pudding mixes	12 months	Keep cool and dry.
Rice, mixes	6 months	Keep cool and dry.
Sauce and gravy mixes	6–12 months	Keep cool and dry.
Soup mixes	12 months	Keep cool and dry.
Toaster pastries	2–3 months	Keep in airtight packet.
Canned and dried foods		
Canned foods, all (unopened)	12 months*	Keep cool.
Canned fruit juices	9 months*	Keep cool.
Canned foods (opened)		*All opened canned foods:*
baby foods	2–3 days	Refrigerate and cover tightly. To avoid metallic taste,
fish and seafood	2 days	transfer foods in cans to
fruit	1 week	glass or plastic storage containers, if kept more than
meats	2 days	1 day.
pickles, olives	1–2 months	
poultry	2 days	
sauce, tomato	5 days	
vegetables	3 days	
Fruits, dried	6 months ⎫	Keep cool, in airtight container; if possible refrigerate.
Vegetables, dried	1 year ⎭	
Spices, herbs, condiments and extracts		
Catsup, chili sauce (unopened)	12 months*	Refrigerate for longer storage.
(opened)	1 month	

CUPBOARD STORAGE CHART (continued)

Food	Recommended storage time at 70° F.	Handling hints
Spices, herbs, condiments and extracts (continued)		
Mustard, prepared yellow		
(unopened)	2 years*	
(opened)	6–8 months	May be refrigerated. Stir before using.
Spices and herbs		
whole spices	1–2 years	Store in airtight containers in dry places away from sunlight and heat. At times listed, check aroma; if faded, replace. Whole cloves, nutmeg and cinnamon sticks maintain quality beyond 2-year period.
ground spices	6 months	
herbs	6 months	
herb/spice blends	6 months	
Vanilla		
(unopened)	2 years*	
(opened)	12 months	Keep tightly closed. Volatile oils escape.
other extracts		
(opened)	12 months	Keep tightly closed. Volatile oils escape.
Veget., dehyd. flakes	6 months	
Others		
Cheese, parmesan, grated		
(unopened)	10 months*	
(opened)	2 months	Refrigerate after opening. Keep tightly closed.
Coconut, shredded, canned or packaged		
(unopened)	12 months*	
(opened)	6 months	Refrigerate after opening.
Meat substitutes, textured protein products (e.g., imitation bacon bits)	4 months	Keep tightly closed. For longer storage, refrigerate.
Metered-caloric products, instant breakfast	6 months	Keep in can, closed jars or original packets.

CUPBOARD STORAGE CHART (continued)

Food	Recommended storage time at 70° F.	Handling hints
Others (continued)		
Nuts		
in shell (unopened)	4 months*	Refrigerate after opening.
nutmeats packaged (unopened)		Freeze for longer storage. Unsalted and blanched nuts
vacuum can	1 year*	keep longer than salted.
other packaging	3 months*	
nutmeats (opened)	2 weeks	
Peanut butter		
(unopened)	6–9 months*	Refrigeration not needed.
(opened)	2–3 months	Keeps longer if refrigerated. Use at room temperature.
Peas, beans, dried	12 months	Store in airtight container in cool place.
Popcorn	2 years	Store in airtight container.
Vegetables, fresh		
onions	2 weeks	Keep dry and away from
potatoes, white	2 weeks	sun. For longer storage,
sweet	2 weeks	keep at about 50° F. Don't refrigerate sweet potatoes.
Whipped topping (dry)	12 months	Keep cool and dry.
Yeast, dry	Expiration date on package	

SOURCE: Consumer Marketing Information, Cooperative Extension Service, East Lansing: Michigan State University.

* Total time "unopened" product can be stored at home. If recommendation is for "opened" product, subtract this time from the total home storage or "unopened" time.

REFRIGERATOR STORAGE CHART

Temperature: From 34° F. to 40° F. is best. Above 40° F. foods spoil rapidly. *Check temperature with a refrigerator thermometer or an outdoor thermometer.*

Time: Use food quickly—*don't depend on maximum storage time.*

Packaging: Use foil, plastic wrap or bags, airtight containers.

General Care: Clean refrigerator regularly to cut down food odors. Remove spoiled foods immediately so that decay can't be passed to other foods.

Food	Recommended storage time at 37° F.	Handling hints
Dairy products		
Butter	1–2 weeks	Wrap or cover tightly. Hold only 2-day butter supply or 2-week margarine supply in butter keeper.
Margarine	4–6 months	
Buttermilk	3–5 days	Cover tightly. Flavor not affected if buttermilk separates; remix before serving.
Cheese		
cottage, ricotta	5 days	Keep all cheese tightly packaged in moisture-resistant wrap. If outside of hard cheese gets moldy, just cut mold away—it won't affect flavor. For longer storage, see freezer storage chart.
cream, neufchatel	2 weeks	
hard and wax-coated— cheddar, edam, gouda, Swiss, brick, etc. large pieces;		
unopened	3–6 months	
opened	3–4 weeks	
sliced	2 weeks	
parmesan, romano (grated) (opened)	2 months	Refrigerate after opening. (See cupboard storage chart.)
process (opened)	3–4 weeks	Refrigerate slices of process cheese and cheese food. Refrigerate loaves and jars after opened. Most squeeze packages and aerosol cans don't need refrigeration (check label).

REFRIGERATOR STORAGE CHART (continued)

Food	Recommended storage time at 37° F.	Handling hints
Dairy products (continued)		
Cream		
light, heavy, half-and-half	3 days	Cover tightly. To prevent bacteria spreading into leftover cream, don't return unused cream to original container.
Coffee lightener (liquid)	3 weeks	Don't return unused portion to original container.
Dips, sour cream, etc.		
commercial	2 weeks	Keep tightly covered.
homemade	2 days	Keep tightly covered.
Eggs		
in shell	2–3 weeks	Store covered. Keep small end down to center yolks.
whites	3 days	Store in covered container.
yolks	3 days	Cover yolks with water; store in covered container.
Milk		
evaporated (opened)	4–5 days	Keep covered.
homogenized, reconstituted dry nonfat, skimmed	5 days	Keep containers tightly closed. Don't return unused milk to original container.
sweetened, condensed (opened)	4–5 days	Keep covered.
Sour cream	2 weeks	Keep covered.
Whipped topping		
in aerosol can	3 months	
prepared from mix	3 days	Keep covered.
bought frozen (once thawed)	2 weeks	Keep covered.
Yogurt	7–10 days	Keep covered.
Fruits and vegetables—fresh		
Fruit		
bananas		Refrigerate only when fully ripe.

REFRIGERATOR STORAGE CHART (continued)

Food	Recommended storage time at 37° F.	Handling hints
Fruits and vegetables—fresh (continued)		
apples	1–3 weeks	Discard bruised or decayed
berries, cherries	1–2 days	fruit. Don't wash before
citrus fruit	1 week	storing—moisture encourages spoilage. Store in crisper or moisture-resistant bag or wrap.
citrus juice— bottled, reconstituted frozen, canned	6 days	Keep fruit juice tightly covered. Transfer canned juice to glass or plastic container if not used up in 1 day.
melons	1 week	Wrap uncut cantaloupe & honeydew to prevent odor spreading to other foods.
other	3–5 days	Wrap cut surfaces of citrus fruit and cantaloupe to prevent vitamin C loss.
Vegetables		
asparagus, corn in husks	1–2 days	Keep moist.
beans, green or wax	1–2 days	Keep in crisper or moisture-resistant wrap or bag.
beets, carrots, radishes	1–2 weeks	Remove leafy tops; keep in crisper.
cabbage, celery	1–2 weeks	Keep in crisper or moisture resistant wrap or bag.
lettuce, head (unwashed)	5–7 days	Store in moisture-resistant wrap, bag or lettuce keeper.
lettuce, head (washed, thoroughly drained)	3–5 days	Store away from other vegetables and fruits to prevent russet spotting.
mushrooms	1–2 days	Do not wash before storing.
onions, potatoes, sweet potatoes		Refrigeration not needed. See cupboard storage chart.
shredded cabbage, leaf and bibb lettuce, salad greens	1–2 days	Keep in moisture-resistant wrap or bag.

REFRIGERATOR STORAGE CHART (continued)

Food	Recommended storage time at 37° F.	Handling hints
Fruits and vegetables—fresh (continued)		
tomatoes, ripe	1–2 days	Ripen tomatoes at room temperature away from direct sunlight; then refrigerate.
unshelled peas, limas, spinach	3–5 days	Keep in crisper or moisture-resistant wrap or bags.
Meat, fish and poultry—fresh uncooked		
Meats—beef, lamb, pork and veal		*All meat, poultry & fish:*
chops	2–3 days	When bought in plastic
ground meat	1–2 days	wrapping (from self-serve
roasts	2–4 days	counters), store in these
steaks	2–3 days	packages. If not purchased
stew meat	1–2 days	from self-serve counters,
variety meats (liver, heart, etc.)	1 day	remove from package and wrap loosely in waxed paper. This allows surface to
Poultry		dry; dry surface retards
ready-to-cook chicken, duck or turkey	2 days	bacterial growth. (Reason for difference: Meat packages in self-serve counter
Fish and shellfish		have been handled by many
fresh cleaned fish, including steaks and fillets	1 day	shoppers. Opening these before storage provides opportunity for contamina-
Seafood		tion, which more than
including shucked clams, oysters, scallops, shrimp	1 day	offsets merits of "dry surface.") Store in coldest part of refrigerator.
clams, crab, lobster in shell	2 days	Cook only live shellfish.

REFRIGERATOR STORAGE CHART (continued)

Food	Recommended storage time at 37° F.	Handling hints
Cured and smoked meats		
Bacon	5–7 days	Keep wrapped. Store in coldest part of refrigerator or in meat keeper. Times are for opened packages of sliced meats. Unopened vacuum packs keep about 2 weeks.
Bologna loaves, liverwurst	4–6 days	
Corned beef	5–7 days	
Dried beef	10–12 days	
Dry and semi-dry sausage (salami, etc.)	2–3 days	
Frankfurters	4–5 days	
Hams, whole	1 week	
canned (unopened)	6 months	Store in refrigerator unless label indicates refrigeration is not needed.
Liver sausage	4–5 days	
Luncheon meats	3 days	
Sausage, fresh or smoked	2–3 days	
Other foods		
Canned goods		
fruits, opened	1 week	If not used in 1 day, transfer to glass or plastic container to avoid metallic taste. Cover and refrigerate.
vegetables, opened	2–3 days	
puddings, custards (opened)	1–2 days	Keep covered.
Leftover gravy and broth	2 days	Keep covered.
Refrigerated biscuits, rolls, pastries, cookie dough	Expiration date on label	Don't store in refrigerator door; temperature fluctuation and jarring lower quality.

SOURCE: Consumer Marketing Information, Cooperative Extension Service. East Lansing: Michigan State University.

FREEZER STORAGE CHART

Temperature: 0° F. or below is best. Maximum temperature should be 5° F. *Check temperature with freezer thermometer or outdoor thermometer,* or use this rule of thumb: if freezer can't keep ice cream brick-solid, temperature is above the recommended level. In this case, don't store food more than a week.

Time: Date food packages with an "expiration date" according to maximum storage time recommended below. Longer storage is not dangerous, but flavors and textures begin to deteriorate.

Packaging: Use foil, moisture vapor-proof plastic bags and wraps, freezer wrap or freezer containers. Foil, when folded, may develop pinholes, resulting in freezer burn.

Commercial Frozen Foods: Pick up frozen foods just before going to checkout counter. Purchase only foods frozen solid. Place in home freezer as soon as possible. Cook or thaw according to label instructions.

Home Frozen Foods: Freeze in coldest part of freezer. Freeze no more than 3 lbs. per cubic foot of freezer space within 24 hours. Don't freeze a quarter of beef.

Food	Approximate storage time at 0° F.	Handling hints
Meat, fish, poultry		
Meat—home frozen		
bacon[a]		[a] Freezing cured meats not recommended. Saltiness encourages rancidity. If frozen, use within a month.
corned beef[a]		
frankfurters[b]		
ground beef, lamb, veal	2–3 months	
ground pork	1–2 months	
ham and picnic, cured[a]		[b] Freezing not recommended. Emulsion may be broken, and product will "weep."
luncheon meat[b]		
roasts		[c] Freezing alters flavor. Check for holes in trays and plastic wrap of fresh meat. If none, freeze in this wrap up to 2 weeks. For longer storage, overwrap with suitable freezer wrap. Put two layers of waxed paper between individual hamburger patties.
beef	6–12 months	
lamb, veal	6–9 months	
pork	3–6 months	
sausage, dry, smoked[c]		
sausage, fresh, unsalted	1–2 months	
steaks and chops		
beef	6–9 months	
lamb, veal	3–4 months	
pork	2–3 months	
venison, game birds	8–12 months	

FREEZER STORAGE CHART (continued)

Food	Approximate storage time at 0° F.	Handling hints

MEAT, FISH, POULTRY (continued)

Fish—home frozen and purchased frozen

fillets and steaks from "lean" fish:		Same as *Meat—home frozen*
cod, flounder, haddock, sole	6 months	
"fatty" fish: bluefish, perch, mackerel, salmon	2–3 months	
breaded fish	3 months	Keep purchased frozen fish in original wrapping; thaw; follow cooking directions on label.
clams	3 months	
cooked fish or seafood	3 months	
king crab	10 months	
lobster tails	3 months	
oysters	4 months	
scallops	3 months	
shrimp, uncooked	12 months	

Poultry—home frozen or purchased frozen

chicken, whole or cut-up	10 months	Same as *Meat—home frozen*
chicken livers	3 months	
cooked poultry	3 months	
duck, turkey	6 months	

Fruits and vegetables

Fruit—home frozen or purchased frozen

berries, cherries, peaches, pears, pineapple, etc.	12 months	Freeze in moisture vapor-proof container.
citrus fruit and juice frozen at home	6 months	
fruit juice concentrates	12 months	

Vegetables—home frozen or purchased frozen

home frozen	10 months	Cabbage, celery, salad greens and tomatoes do not freeze successfully.
purchased frozen— cartons, plastic bags or boil-in-bags	8 months	

FREEZER STORAGE CHART (continued)

Food	Approximate storage time at 0° F.	Handling hints
Commercial frozen foods		

Also see: meats, fish, poultry; fruits, vegetables; dairy products.

Baked goods

Food	Approximate storage time at 0° F.	Handling hints
yeast bread and rolls, baked	3–6 months	
rolls, partially baked	2–3 months	
bread, unbaked	1 month	
quick bread, baked	2-3 months	
cake, baked, unfrosted		
angel food	2 months	Freezing does not freshen baked goods. It can only maintain the quality (freshness) the food had before freezing.
chiffon, sponge	2 months	
cheese cake	2–3 months	
chocolate	4 months	
fruit cake	12 months	
yellow or pound	6 months	
caked, baked, frosted	8–12 months	
cookies, baked	8–12 months	
pie, baked	1–2 months	
fruit pie, unbaked	8 months	

Main dishes

Food	Approximate storage time at 0° F.	Handling hints
meat, fish, poultry pies and casseroles	3 months	
TV dinners		
shrimp, ham, pork, frankfurter	3 months	
beef, turkey, chicken, fish	6 months	

Home frozen foods

Also see: meats, fish, poultry; fruits, vegetables; dairy products.

Food	Approximate storage time at 0° F.	Handling hints
Bread	3 months	
Cake	3 months	Package foods tightly in foil, moisture vapor-proof plastic wrap, freezer wrap or watertight freezer containers. For casseroles, allow head room for expansion.
Casseroles—meat, fish, poultry	3 months	
Cookies, baked and dough	3 months	
Nuts		
salted	6–8 months	
unsalted	9–12 months	
Pies, unbaked fruit	8 months	

FREEZER STORAGE CHART (continued)

Food	Approximate storage time at 0° F.	Handling hints
Dairy products		
Butter	6–9 months	Store in moisture vapor-proof freezer container or wrap.
Margarine	12 months	
Whipped butter and margarine		Do not freeze. Emulsion will break, and product will separate.
Buttermilk, sour cream, and yogurt		Do not freeze.
Cheese		
camembert	3 months	Thaw in refrigerator.
cottage, farmer cheese (dry curd only)	3 months	Thaw in refrigerator. Do not freeze creamed cottage cheese—it gets mushy.
neufchatel		Do not freeze.
hard cheese		Cut and wrap cheese in small pieces. When frozen, may show mottled color due to surface moisture. Thaw in refrigerator.
cheddar	6 weeks	
edam, gouda, Swiss, brick, etc.	6–8 weeks	
process cheese food products (loaf, slices)	4 months	
roquefort, blue	3 months	Becomes crumbly after thawing. Still good for salads and melting.
Cream—light, heavy, half-and-half	2 months	Heavy cream may not whip after thawing. Use for cooking. Thaw in refrigerator.
whipped	1 month	Make whipped cream dollops; freeze firm. Place in plastic bag or carton; seal; store in freezer. To thaw, place on top of dessert.
Eggs		
in shell		Do not freeze.
whites	12 months	Store in covered container. Freeze in amounts for specific recipes.

FREEZER STORAGE CHART (continued)

Food	Approximate storage time at 0° F.	Handling hints
Eggs (continued)		
yolks	12 months	For sweet dishes, mix each cup yolks with 1 tablespoon corn syrup or sugar. For other cooking, substitute ½ teaspoon salt for sugar.
Ice cream, ice milk, sherbet	2 months	Cover with plastic wrap or foil after each use to prevent drying out.
Milk	1 month	Allow room for expansion in freezer container. Thaw in refrigerator. Freezing affects flavor and appearance. Use in cooking and baking.

SOURCE: Consumer Marketing Information, Cooperative Extension Service, East Lansing: Michigan State University.

A DAILY FOOD GUIDE

Meat Group

Foods Included

Beef, veal, lamb, pork, variety meats such as liver, heart, kidney.
Poultry and eggs
Fish and shellfish
As alternates—dry beans, dry peas, lentils, nuts, peanuts, peanut butter

Amounts Recommended

Choose 2 or more servings every day.
Count as a serving: 2 to 3 ounces of lean cooked meat, poultry, or fish —all without bone; 2 eggs; 1 cup cooked dry beans, dry peas, or lentils; 4 tablespoons peanut butter.

Vegetable-Fruit Group

Foods Included

All vegetables and fruits. This guide emphasizes those that are valuable as sources of vitamin C and vitamin A.

Sources of Vitamin C

Good sources—grapefruit or grapefruit juice, orange or orange juice, cantaloupe, guava, mango, papaya, raw strawberries, broccoli, brussels sprouts, green pepper, sweet red pepper

Fair sources—honeydew melon, lemon, tangerine or tangerine juice, watermelon, asparagus tips, raw cabbage, collards, garden cress, kale, kohlrabi, mustard greens, potatoes and sweet potatoes, cooked in the jacket, spinach, tomatoes or tomato juice, turnip greens.

Sources of Vitamin A

Dark-green and deep-yellow vegetables and a few fruits, namely, apricots, broccoli, cantaloupe, carrots, chard, collards, cress, kale, mango, persimmon, pumpkin, spinach, sweet potatoes, turnip greens and other dark-green leaves, winter squash.

Amounts Recommended

Choose 4 or more servings every day, including:

1 serving of a good source of vitamin C or 2 servings of a fair source.

1 serving at least every other day, of a good source of vitamin A. If the food chosen for vitamin C is also a good source of vitamin A, the additional serving of a vitamin A food may be omitted.

The remaining 1 to 3 or more servings may be of any vegetable or fruit, including those that are valuable for vitamin C and for vitamin A.

Count as 1 serving: ½ cup of vegetable or fruit; or a portion as ordinarily served, such as 1 medium apple, banana, orange, or potato, half a medium grapefruit or cantaloupe, or the juice of 1 lemon.

SOURCE: U.S. Department of Agriculture.

Milk Group

Foods Included

Milk—fluid whole, evaporated, skim, dry, buttermilk
Cheese—cottage; cream; cheddar-type, natural or process
Ice cream

Amounts Recommended

Some milk every day for everyone.

Recommended amounts are given below in terms of 8-ounce cups of whole fluid milk:

Children under 9	2 to 3	Adults	2 or more
Children 9 to 12	3 or more	Pregnant women	3 or more
Teenagers	4 or more	Nursing mothers	4 or more

Part or all of the milk may be fluid skim milk, buttermilk, evaporated milk, or dry milk.

Cheese and ice cream may replace part of the milk. The amount of either it will take to replace a given amount of milk is figured on the basis of calcium content. Common portions of cheese and of ice cream and their milk equivalents in calcium are:

1-inch cube cheddar-type cheese	=½ cup milk
½ cup cottage cheese	=⅓ cup milk
2 tablespoons cream cheese	=1 tablespoon milk
½ cup ice cream	=¼ cup milk

Bread-Cereal Group

Foods Included

All breads and cereals that are whole grain, enriched, or restored; *check labels to be sure.*

Specifically, this group includes breads; cooked cereals; ready-to-eat cereals; cornmeal; crackers; flour; grits; macaroni and spaghetti; noodles; rice; rolled oats; and quick breads and other baked goods if made with whole-grain or enriched flour. Bulgur and parboiled rice and wheat also may be included in this group.

Amounts Recommended

Choose 4 servings or more daily. Or, if no cereals are chosen, have an extra serving of breads or baked goods, which will make at least 5 servings from this group daily.

Count as 1 serving: 1 slice of bread; 1 ounce ready-to-eat cereal; ½ to ¾ cup cooked cereal, cornmeal, grits, macaroni, noodles, rice, or spaghetti.

Other Foods

To round out meals and meet energy needs, almost everyone will use some foods not specified in the four food groups. Such foods include unenriched, refined breads, cereals, flours; sugars; butter, margarine, other fats. These often are ingredients in a recipe or added to other foods during preparation or at the table.

Try to include some vegetable oil among the fats used.